ACTS

LIVING WITH PASSIONATE FAITH

JUDSON EDWARDS

Annual
Bible
Study

Study Guide

SMYTH&HELWYS
PUBLISHING INCORPORATED · MACON, GEORGIA

CONTENTS

Annual Bible Study

Cecil P. Staton, Jr.
President & CEO

Lex Horton
Publisher / Executive Vice
President

P. Keith Gammons
Vice President, Production

Leslie Andres
Editor

Kelley F. Land
Assistant Editor

Betsy Butler
Associate Editor

Wesley Crook
Dave Jones
Graphic Design

Cover art
(Credit: Statue of Paul, Todd Bolen,
BiblePlaces.com)

Sidebar material has been adapted
from J. Bradley Chance, *Acts*,
Smyth & Helwys Bible Commentary
(Macon GA: Smyth & Helwys, 2007).

1-800-747-3016 (USA)
1-800-568-1248 (Canada)

PUBLISHING INCORPORATED   MACON GEORGIA
WWW.HELWYS.COM

GATHERING A COMMUNITY (ACTS 1–5)

Focal Text—Acts 2:42-47

The first thing I did after agreeing to write this study on the book of Acts was to sit down and read Acts from beginning to end. I was on vacation in Oregon, so I took my Bible down to the Alsea River, sat in a folding chair, and, with only the sound of the river gurgling in the background, read Acts. When I finished my reading, I found myself trying to untangle a jumble of feelings.

I felt *intrigue* because I read things I had either never read before or maybe had read and forgotten. I felt *confusion* because the Acts world of speaking in tongues, communicating with angels, and healing people physically seemed so foreign to my world. I felt *admiration* because those first Christians were so tenacious and resilient. I felt *embarrassment* because their faith seemed so much stronger than mine. But mostly I felt *enthusiasm* because of the example of those first believers. The book of Acts is about passionate faith, and just reading it from beginning to end gave me a new injection of passion.

THE FLOW OF THE STORY

Reading Acts in its entirety also helped me realize the "flow" of the book, how Luke logically moves in his writing from one "thought compartment" to the next. It seemed to me that the book of Acts unfolds in an easy-to-outline form that includes four distinct sections.

The first section, chapters 1 through 5, is about *gathering a community*. In this section, Luke tells us how the early church organized itself, how the Holy Spirit energized those believers, and how they grew to love one another. By the end of the fifth chapter, the early church is in place, and its trademark is a white-hot fire of enthusiasm.

The next section in Acts, which includes chapters 6 through 15, is about *breaking down walls.* Luke shows us one incident after another where the early believers moved beyond provincialism to share the good news with the whole world. By the end of chapter 15, many walls have been demolished, and the church has made itself clear: Jesus is for everyone!

Logically, then, the next section of Acts, chapters 16 through 20, is about *spreading the word.* This section focuses primarily on the Apostle Paul as he travels throughout the ancient world declaring the good news of Jesus.

The final section of Acts, which encompasses chapters 21 through 28, is about *taking a stand.* In this final section of the book, Paul is again the focal point—only now he is trapped in prison. From prison cells in Jerusalem, Caesarea, and Rome, Paul takes a stand before a crowd in Jerusalem, the Sanhedrin, and a succession of government leaders: Felix, Festus, and Agrippa.

Gathering a community. Breaking down walls. Spreading the word. Taking a stand. Those four phrases capture the essence of the book of Acts and will serve as the outline for our study. Each section also includes a focal passage that gets special attention and especially captures the theme of that section. We begin by examining the first five chapters of Acts and seeing how the early Christians gathered a community of faith.

JESUS GIVES FINAL INSTRUCTIONS AND ASCENDS TO HEAVEN (1:1-11)

Luke addressed the book of Acts to a man named Theophilus. No one knows who Theophilus was, and some scholars even suggest that the name is a generic one referring to no particular person at all. Theophilus, in Greek, means "lover of God," so Luke might have been addressing his book to all lovers of God. The Gospel of Luke is also addressed to Theophilus, which gives further credence to the notion that Luke wrote both books.

After greeting Theophilus, Luke quickly ushers Jesus onto the stage of his drama. He had written about Jesus "in the first book," he says, and now he is going to continue the story.

The first words Jesus utters in Acts are, "This is what you have heard from me; for John baptized with water, but you will be baptized with the Holy Spirit not many days from now" (Acts 1:5). The disciples barely heard those words. They were so intent on being a part of something grand and glorious that they had their minds elsewhere: "Lord, is this the time when you will restore the kingdom to Israel?" (Acts 1:6).

Remember, the people of Israel had always seen the Messiah as a political leader who would lead them back to prominence. For some 600 years, Israel had been ruled by other nations, and the people craved a Messiah who could restore their independence and glory. The disciples' question to Jesus revealed that old mentality about the Messiah. It also revealed the extent to which they were still in the dark about the true meaning of Jesus and his kingdom. What Jesus meant by "kingdom of God" and what they meant by "kingdom of God" were miles apart.

Jesus told them it was not for them to know "the times or the periods that the Father has set by his own authority" (Acts 1:7). Some things would not be revealed to them, and they needed to know that. Though they would get *some* revelation, they would not get *total* revelation. Don't most of us eventually find ourselves face to face with our limitations? Like those early Christians, we're filled with "when" and "why" questions for God but can't get satisfactory answers. More and more, along the Christian Way, we find ourselves admitting our ignorance and leaning into the sovereignty of a good God.

But Jesus told those early followers that there was something they *could* know and do: they were to wait for the Holy Spirit to come upon them and receive the Spirit's power, and then they were to be witnesses for Christ in Jerusalem, in all Judea and Samaria, and to the ends of the earth. They were not responsible for *everything*, but they were responsible for *something*.

It is worth noting that the coming of the Spirit was connected primarily to the task of bearing witness to the world. The early believers were to receive the power of the Spirit not to get an ecstatic experience or emotional high, but to take the good news of Jesus and his resurrection to other people. The Holy Spirit came to give them power to serve, pray, preach, give, and go. It was not the power to *feel* something so much as it was the power to *do* something.

After issuing his marching orders to the early followers, Jesus ascended to heaven. By verse 11 in the Acts story, Jesus has bodily left the earth, and the implication is clear: the baton has been passed to this ragtag bunch of ordinary people. If the Way of Jesus is going to infect the world, it will be because these people form a community of witnesses that will serve, pray, preach, give, and go. After just eleven verses in Acts, Jesus has departed, and the spotlight has shifted to the community.

THE APOSTLES CHOOSE A REPLACEMENT FOR JUDAS (1:12-26)

Peter, the acknowledged leader of the group of 120 believers, stood to speak and announced that a replacement for Judas was needed. This was, after all, a distinctly Jewish community with a mission to the people of Israel. The twelve tribes of Israel needed twelve witnesses, thus the concern to find a twelfth apostle. Peter set the entire experience in the context of Scripture and God's sovereignty. Even the defection and death of Judas, he said, were predicted by David in the Psalms.

The qualification for the new apostle was this: he had to be "one of the men who have accompanied us during all the time that the Lord Jesus went in and out among us, beginning from the baptism of John until the day when he was taken up from us" (Acts 1:21-22). Two men, Justus and Matthias, met that qualification and were nominated. After the group prayed, the group "cast lots," which probably meant they put both names on stones, put the stones in a container, and shook the container until one stone came out. The stone that popped out read "Matthias," and the new apostle had been chosen.

Casting Lots

A traditional means within Judaism to determine God's will (see Lev 16:8; Num 26:55-56; 33:54; Josh 19:1-40; 1 Chr 26:12-16; Mic 2:5; Jonah 1:7-8), the practice of casting lots was also employed at Qumran. Stones were marked to designate certain persons and placed in a jar or a bag. The container was shaken until a stone fell out determining the one on whom "the lot fell." Chance was viewed as divinely determined: "Before Pentecost, before the presence of the Spirit to lead it, the church sought the direction of God and used the Old Testament procedure of securing divine decision" (Polhill, 95).

John B. Polhill, *Acts* (NAC 26; Nashville: Broadman, 1992).

Several things stand out in this process of choosing the new member of the Twelve: (1) The new apostle had to be an eyewitness to the life of Jesus. Credibility was crucial. (2) The process involved the whole community. Peter proposed the need, but the community was involved in the decision. (3) The new apostle was chosen through discernment *and* prayer. Both human wisdom *and* divine wisdom were involved in the process. (4) The casting of lots seems strange to us but was a common Jewish way of discerning the will of God. It is worth noting that this is the last time this practice is mentioned in Scripture. After Pentecost, the Christians used the guidance of the Holy Spirit.

When the curtain closes on chapter 1 of Acts, then, two significant things have happened. First, after giving his followers orders to be his witnesses to the world, Jesus has ascended to heaven. The baton has been passed to the community. Second, the community has begun to get its leadership in place. A replacement for Judas has been found, and, in the process, the community has established a pattern for making decisions.

But what happened next sent shock waves throughout that band of 120 Christians. In fact, it sent shock waves throughout *history.*

THE HOLY SPIRIT COMES AT PENTECOST (2:1-13)

Pentecost was one of three great festivals that all Jewish males were expected to attend in Jerusalem (see pages 89 and 90, **Jerusalem in the First Century** and **Map of Jerusalem**). The three festivals were Passover, Tabernacles, and Pentecost (called "the feast of weeks" in the Old Testament). Pentecost commemorated the completion of the grain harvest, and some think it was the most popular feast of the Jewish year. Ordinarily, Pentecost fell within the last two weeks of May.

But no one could have predicted what would happen at that particular festival of Pentecost. The 120 Christians were all together in one place. Suddenly, they heard the sound of rushing wind, as if a tornado were descending upon them. They saw what looked like tongues of fire snapping and cracking around them and landing on each of them. Then they began to speak in other languages so that foreigners among them could understand what they were saying. As Luke recorded it, "All were amazed and perplexed, saying to one another, 'What does this mean?'" (Acts 2:12).

It was a breathtaking, life-changing experience—the kind of experience, frankly, that we would all like to have. When wind blows and fire falls, we don't have to walk by faith; we get to walk by sight. I can't tell you how many times I've prayed for a Pentecost experience or a Damascus Road experience like Saul of Tarsus had. I'm guessing I'm not the only person yearning for those obvious, dramatic experiences with God that remove all doubt from our minds. If only we could have a Pentecost, we would amaze people with our dynamic faith!

How do we put Luke's account of Pentecost in perspective? I am content to take it exactly as he described it. How much of Luke's account is history and how much is poetry is hard to say, but I am content to believe it happened as he described it. Wind blew, tongues of fire fell, and the believers spoke in languages that strangers from faraway places could understand.

But I also believe Pentecost is not a normative experience for Christians. New Testament scholar Curtis Vaughan writes, "The advent of the Spirit, like the incarnation of God in Christ, had a once-for-all character. Pentecost, then, is as unrepeatable as the birth of Christ or as his death and resurrection."[1] I don't doubt at all that a miracle happened at Pentecost. I do doubt, however, that I should spend much time praying for a Pentecost of my own.

St. Peter Preaching to the Multitude

Masolino da Panicale (1383–1447). *St. Peter Preaching to the Multitude*. (Post-restoration). Brancacci Chapel, S. Maria del Carmine, Florence, Italy. (Credit: Scala / Art Resource, NY)

PETER PREACHES A SERMON AT PENTECOST (2:14-41)

The book of Acts is full of sermons. Its twenty-eight sermons and speeches, given mostly by Peter and Paul, make up one-third of the entire book. Peter preached the first of those just after the miracle at Pentecost.

C. H. Dodd says that Peter's sermon at Pentecost is typical of the sermons preached in Acts, that it follows a pattern that is fairly consistent in apostolic preaching. If we were to look at Peter's sermon notes, his outline might appear something like this:

(1) The age of fulfillment, or the coming of the kingdom of God, is at hand. (Acts 2:16-21)

(2) This coming has taken place through the ministry, death, and resurrection of Jesus. (Acts 2:22-23)

(3) By virtue of the resurrection, Jesus is exalted at the right hand of God as messianic head of the new Israel. (Acts 2:24-36)

(4) The Holy Spirit in the church is the sign of Christ's present power and glory. (Acts 2:33)

(5) Forgiveness, the Holy Spirit, and salvation come with repentance. (Acts 2:38-39)[2]

Though Peter does not mention it in this sermon, many of the speeches/sermons in Acts also include a word about the second coming of Christ. Dodd, in describing Peter's sermon at Pentecost, concludes, "We may take it that this is what the author of Acts meant by 'preaching the kingdom of God.'"[3]

After the sermon, the people who heard it were "cut to the heart" and wanted to know what they should do. Peter told them to repent and be baptized, and 3,000 of them did exactly that. They repented, were baptized, and were added to the church. That little community of faith that had numbered 120 people was little no more.

THE EARLY CHRISTIANS ENCOURAGE ONE ANOTHER (2:42-27)

When I read Acts there by the river in Oregon, I noticed that Luke didn't give many biographical details about any particular person. I learned a few things about Peter, Paul, Stephen, and Philip, but mostly I learned about this new community that had gathered around the cross and resurrection. Luke was not preoccupied with any one individual; he was preoccupied with the church—how that community was formed and how it behaved.

All that we've seen thus far has been a prelude to our focal text. Luke's account of Jesus' ascension and the giving of the marching orders to the church, his description of the community's choosing of Matthias, his depiction of the whirlwind events at Pentecost, and his meticulous recording of Peter's sermon after those events simply set the table for his concise but moving description of the community of Jesus' people. In Acts 2:42-47 and then again in Acts 4:32-37, Luke provides us vivid pictures of the community of faith. His pictures show the early church was marked by six specific characteristics.

First, the early church was a learning community. "They devoted themselves to the apostles' teaching" (Acts 2:42), Luke reports, and it's easy to understand why. All of this information about Jesus—who he was, what he said and did, how he died and rose from the dead—was new information to these people. They were starting from square one in their understanding of the Jesus Way and had to be schooled as kindergartners. In the book of Acts, Luke uses the Greek term *hoi mathetai* ("disciples," "learners," "pupils") twenty-two times to describe the church. Those people had a lot to learn, and they knew it.

This learning dimension of community life is just as important in our day as it was in theirs. In fact, I'm not so sure our culture is much beyond the kindergarten stage in *its* understanding of Jesus and his way.

Stephen Prothero, who has written *Religious Literacy: What Every American Needs to Know—And Doesn't,* confirms my fears. In a chapter titled "Eden (What We Once Knew)," he says, "Once upon a time, Americans were people of the book,"[4] and then proceeds to document the fact that they no longer are. Pollster George Barna reports, "The younger a person is, the less they understand about the Christian faith."[5] The chances are good that your children and grandchildren will know less about the Bible and the Jesus Way than you do.

That means that those of us in the church have some work to do. Like the early church, we need to "devote ourselves to the apostles' teaching" and make sure people know the basics of the faith. We still need to focus on being a learning community.

Second, the early church was a worshiping community. In this snapshot of the church in Acts 2, Luke tells us that the church devoted itself to prayer, spent much time in the temple, and praised God together. Though the early believers were not learned theologians, they did know that they had experienced something profound in Christ that needed to be celebrated. So, they did what all Christian communities have done since that day: they worshiped God.

Years ago, I heard a definition of worship that has stayed with me through the years: *Worship is giving the best you have and the best you are to the Best you know.* Those early followers of Jesus did precisely that. They brought themselves and their possessions and offered them to the God who had given them new life in Christ.

Third, the early church was a celebrating community. Luke's description of the first church makes us envious of the kind of *esprit de corp* they had. He reports that "they broke bread at home and ate their food with glad and generous hearts" (Acts 2:46). Their life together was marked by praise for God and a self-sacrificing love for one another. You get the feeling when you read the Acts 2 text, and its companion passage in Acts 4, that this was a fun and exciting community. They celebrated life and the good news of Jesus together.

The Breaking of Bread

This was not a common phrase to denote eating, though the Jewish custom of breaking bread to begin a meal may lie behind the term. Perhaps due to Jesus' act of "breaking bread" in the context of the Passover meal, which was also the "Last Supper" shared between Jesus and his followers, the phrase came to represent for many early Christians meals that they shared with one another in the context of Christian fellowship. In this fellowship the presence of the risen Lord would be at the table. As time went on, the celebration of the Eucharist, or Lord's Supper, came to be separated from the context of "ordinary meals," and the phrase "breaking of bread" becomes synonymous with this ritual Communion meal.

This concept of a celebrating community is in jeopardy in our day because we have privatized faith. We have so focused on the personal dimension of faith that we have neglected the communal dimension.

In Woody Allen's movie *Hannah and Her Sisters,* Woody plays a man wracked by guilt and self-doubt. In his misery, he decides to give Jesus a try and makes a visit to a priest to find out more information. We see Woody staggering away from that meeting with an armload of books. He will approach Jesus individually, through reading. Nowhere in the movie is there anything that looks like a community. Christianity is portrayed as an individual, even solitary, venture. Evidently if you find Jesus at all, you find him alone.

The book of Acts knows nothing of Lone Ranger Christians meeting Jesus in private. It is all about people meeting Jesus in a community and then celebrating that discovery together.

Fourth, the early church was an awestruck community. "Awe came upon everyone, because many signs and wonders were being done by the apostles" (Acts 2:43). That first Christian community was filled with wonder. Six times in Acts, Luke uses the Greek word *existanai,* which translates into "astonished" or "amazed." Church for them was not "old hat" but something fresh and exciting.

Calvin Miller once wrote,

Christianity came alive in the first century in a "What's Next" context:

I won a charioteer while a hitchhiker! What's next?

I healed a cripple and he ran at the temple gate. What's next?

I preached, I did it. Me! I preached. I can't preach, but I preached. Three thousand were saved! What's next?

I raised the dead. What's next?

When I ask, "What's next?" I get such answers as "the Sweetheart Banquet" or "the Forward Program." Nobody has to guess what's next: We keep it mimeographed one year ahead. There is nothing inscrutable about us. Nothing unpredictable. Nothing mysterious. Worship and practice seem always the same.[6]

The church as Luke depicts it in Acts was inscrutable, unpredictable, mysterious, and absolutely filled with awe at what God was doing among them.

Fifth, the early church was a generous community. Actually, that's putting it mildly. Those early believers were *extremely* generous. In Acts 2:44 it says that "all who believed were together and had all things in common; they would sell their possessions and goods and distribute the proceeds to all, as any had need." In chapter 4, Luke mentions again that the early believers held their possessions in common and adds this note: "There was not a needy person among them, for as many as owned lands or houses sold them and brought the proceeds of what was sold. They laid it at the apostles' feet, and it was distributed to each as any had need" (Acts 4:34-35).

Communal Society

"The belongings of friends are held in common." Greek Proverb

In the second chapter of Acts the mystical and the practical sit side by side. Acts 2 begins with wind, fire, and strange tongues and ends with people sharing their goods so that no one would be hungry or homeless. Both the mystical and the practical are part of the church's calling. We deal with mystery and Spirit and holy truths, but we also deal with practical issues like hunger and homelessness. The first church took that mystical experience at Pentecost and translated it into an almost unbelievable and supremely practical generosity.

Sixth, the early church was a contagious community. Life in the New Testament world was not fun. The Roman Empire ruled the nation with an iron fist, and people chafed under its oppressive rule. Few people felt free and prosperous. Add to that the oppressive religion of the scribes and Pharisees that

Jesus so adamantly opposed, and you see another reason that life was dismal. In first-century Judaism, a life with God had been reduced to a long list of boring rules and obligatory rituals. There was no zest or vitality in the religious system. Legalism had strangled all hope.

It's not difficult to see why the early church was able to make such an impact in that world. Imagine in that discouraging world of political and religious oppression how refreshing the early church would seem—a learning, worshiping, celebrating, awestruck, generous group of people. They would shine like lights in the darkness, and they would attract a following. Luke says they had the goodwill of all the people, and "day by day the Lord added to their number those who were being saved" (Acts 2:47). In a toxic culture, here was fresh air! And people came in droves to breathe its life-giving fragrance.

The church is the place where people can breathe fresh air. At church, people can hear about a God who loves them, a Jesus who died and rose for them, and a Spirit who lives within them to give them joy. At church, people can plug into a community that is learning, worshiping, celebrating, awestruck, and generous and see a whole new way of coming at life. In short, at church, people can catch the scent of grace, which is the best antidote for the poison of the world.

After sketching that delightful picture of the early church, Luke then turns his attention to what that community *does*. Chapters 3, 4, and 5 of Acts focus on the question, "What does the community of faith do?" and Luke shows us the community in action.

PETER AND JOHN HEAL A CRIPPLED MAN (3:1-10)

Luke first tells us that this community—or at least certain members of this community—could bring the healing power of Jesus to sick people. A man at the Beautiful Gate, who was crippled and begging for alms, called out to Peter and John for money. Peter responded by saying he didn't have silver and gold to give him (after all, this community had all things in common), but that he could offer him something else: "In the name of Jesus Christ of Nazareth, stand up and walk" (Acts 3:6). The man was healed, jumped up, and began leaping for joy. The bystanders, understandably, were filled with wonder and amazement.

Beautiful Gate

Christian tradition has associated the Beautiful Gate with the Shushan Gate. This would be the gate closest to the viewer in the image of the temple labeled "The Inner Courts." But this gate accommodated the least traffic, and one can see from the map of Jerusalem that it would make no sense for Peter and John, if they were living in Jerusalem itself, to enter through this gate, as there were numerous other gates located to the south and north to allow entrance into the inner courts. Josephus describes a massive "Corinthian Gate" as that separating the Court of Women from the Court of Priests. In the image it is the gate located in the middle of the picture, with large steps leading up to it. Note the close-up in the second image below.

This may be a more a logical place for a lame man to be set and is the gate through which Peter and John would have *had* to pass to enter the courts for the afternoon prayer/offering service. It is reasonable, therefore, to imagine this "Corinthian Gate" as the equivalent for Acts' "Beautiful Gate," despite Christian tradition. One cannot be absolutely sure, for only Acts makes reference to a "Beautiful Gate." Further, Acts itself creates confusion, for if the Beautiful Gate is the gate within the inner court, v. 11 shifts immediately to Solomon's Portico. Note that Solomon's Portico is located *outside* the inner courts. The Western text, however, clears up this potential confusion. It reads: "He entered with them into the temple and all the people saw him . . . and when Peter and John went out he went with them, holding on to them, and (the people) stood in amazement in the Porch called Solomon's" (Lake, 484).

Kirsopp Lake, "Localities In and Near Jerusalem Mentioned in Acts: The Beautiful Gate," in F. J. Foakes Jackson and Kirsopp Lake, *The Beginnings of Christianity: The Acts of the Apostles*, 5 vols. (Grand Rapids MI: Baker, 1979), 5.479–86.

The Inner Courts

The Inner Courts. Model of Jerusalem. Holy Land Hotel, Jerusalem. (Credit: Jim Pitts)

Beautiful Gate Detail

Beautiful Gate. Model of Jerusalem. Holy Land Hotel, Jerusalem. (Credit: Jim Pitts)

Luke would have us know that this community that learns, worships, and celebrates—this community that is awestruck, generous, and contagious—in no way avoids the misery of crippled beggars. It confronts the suffering of the world head-on and offers it the healing power of Jesus.

PETER ADDRESSES THE CROWD (3:11-26)

That healing provided Peter the opportunity to preach the gospel to this astonished crowd. The message, his second in Acts, was blunt and confrontational: "You rejected the Holy and Righteous One and asked to have a murderer given to you, and you killed the Author of life, whom God raised from the dead. To this we are witnesses" (Acts 3:14-15). Their only hope was to "repent therefore and turn to God so that your sins may be wiped out" (Acts 3:19). This community would also be bold in confronting evil and speaking the truth.

Titles for Jesus in Acts 3:14-15

AΩ *Holy One*. The term "the Holy One" (*ho hagion*) was a designation for Jesus in the Synoptic tradition (Mark 1:24 and par.), the Johannine tradition (John 6:69; 1 John 2:20), and in the Apocalypse (Rev 3:7). Acts uses the phrase three times, twice when quoting the LXX (2:27; 13:35, which uses the Greek word *hosios*) and 3:14. Luke also uses *hagion* attributively in Acts 4:27 and 30 ("holy servant/child"). The term is not a "christological" or "messianic" title per se, but it does designate Jesus as one who belongs to and is set apart by God, making his murder particularly heinous.

Righteous One. Only in Acts is the adjective "righteous" used substantively with reference to Jesus: "the Righteous One" (3:14; 7:52; 22:14). The substantive use implies that the adjective is used as a title, not only as an indicator of Jesus' character. *The Similitudes of Enoch* use "the Righteous One" as a designation for the Messiah (38:2), but this does not allow the conclusion that it was a formal messianic title in Judaism. Not only do many question the pre-Christian dating of the *Similitudes*, but also one example hardly makes for a formal title. As "the Righteous One" Jesus was, therefore, totally undeserving of death (precisely the point of Luke 23:43, which uses the word *dikaios*); fittingly, it is through this One that people can, themselves, be made "righteous" (13:38-39; translated as "set free" in the NRSV).

Author of Life. There are four references to this term in the New Testament: Acts 3:15; 5:31; Heb 2:10; 12:2. The term can mean either "leader" or "originator." In ancient literature the latter sense (originator) could denote (quasi-) divine founders of communities or colonies; hence, Jesus may be portrayed as the "founder" of the Christian community. I. H. Marshall believes "originator" works well with Acts 3:15 and Heb 2:10, while "leader" works best with Acts 5:31 and Heb 12:2 (Marshall, 91–92).

I. Howard Marshall, *The Acts of the Apostles: An Introduction and Commentary* (TNTC; Leicester: Inter-Varsity Press, 1984).

PETER AND JOHN ARE ARRESTED
AND SPEAK TO THE AUTHORITIES (4:1-31)

Such boldness would only stir up opposition, and Peter and John were arrested for their preaching. That preaching, however, did not fall on deaf ears: "Many of those who heard the word believed; and they numbered about five thousand" (Acts 4:4).

The next day the religious leaders brought Peter and John before them and demanded, "By what power or by what name do you do this?" (Acts 4:7). That was all the opening Peter needed once again to say a word about Jesus and the fact that Jesus had healed the man at the Beautiful Gate. The religious leaders were amazed at the boldness of these "uneducated and ordinary men" and couldn't refute the fact that the crippled man, healed and happy, was standing right there beside them. They threatened Peter and John and warned them to remain silent, and then released them.

Peter and John went to their Christian friends and told them all that had happened, and they all prayed for even more boldness. The prayer worked: "When they had prayed, the place in which they were gathered together was shaken; and they were all filled with the Holy Spirit and spoke the word of God with boldness" (Acts 4:31). This community was proving itself to be most resilient. Try as they might, the religious authorities couldn't keep these people silent.

THE EARLY CHRISTIANS SHARE THEIR GOODS
WITH EACH OTHER (4:32-37)

Luke has already shown us in our focal passage in Acts 2:42-47 that the early church was extremely generous. In this passage, he underscores that generosity—"there was not a needy person among them"—and then gives an example of one who especially embodied this generosity. Joseph was his name, but the disciples had nicknamed him "Barnabas," which means "son of encouragement." Barnabas, a native of Cyprus and not a Jew by birth, had joined the new Jesus movement and became a model of sacrificial giving. To ensure that there were no needy people among them, Barnabas sold a field and brought the money and laid it at the apostles' feet. Luke wants us to know that this community is generous and focuses on the least, the last, and the lost.

PETER CONFRONTS ANANIAS
AND SAPPHIRA (5:1-11)

If Barnabas was the model of generosity, Ananias and his wife, Sapphira, were the models of stinginess and deception. The early church was mostly generous, for sure, but it was not perfect, and Luke would have us meet a married couple who exemplify that imperfection.

Barnabas, the positive model, sold some land and brought the money to the apostles. Ananias, the negative model, did the same thing, but held some of the money back. He brought only a part of the proceeds to the apostles. When Peter confronted him about his deception, Ananias fell down and died.

Three hours later, his wife, Sapphira, came in, not knowing what had happened to her husband. When she repeated the same deception, Peter confronted her, and she fell down at his feet and died too.

Integrity

Stephen L. Carter says that integrity "requires three steps: (1) *discerning* what is right and what is wrong; (2) *acting* on what you have discerned, even at personal cost; and (3) *saying openly* that you are acting on your understanding of right from wrong" (7).

Ananias and Sapphira offer a clear contrast with the apostles on the issue of integrity. These two people failed to discern what was right, acted instead on what was wrong, and then failed to say openly (and honestly) what they had done. In contrast, the apostles discerned that it was "right" to obey God and speak in the name of Jesus, acted on this belief at great personal risk, and openly declared their intentions and motives to their interrogators.

Stephen L. Carter, *Integrity* (New York: Basic Books, 1996).

This Ananias and Sapphira saga is a strange and shocking story, and one that doesn't lend itself to easy interpretation. I don't know exactly why this couple had to die for their sin, but let me make three comments about this text.

First, Luke doesn't say that God struck them down; he just says they fell over and died after being confronted by Peter. The story may say more about the fear and awe people had for Peter and the other apostles than it does about the punitive nature of God.

Second, the early community of Christians did feel a special need to protect their life together. It would have been easy to go back to the old way—the way of self-gain and lying—and forget about this new way of Jesus. Ananias and Sapphira had to be confronted to make sure the integrity of the group was protected. Stanley Hauerwas and William Willimon, in their book *Resident Aliens,* write, "The church was called to be a colony, an alternative community, a sign, a signal to the world that Christ had made possible a way of life together unlike anything the world had seen. *Not* to confront lies and deceit, greed and self-service among people like Ananias and Sapphira would be the death of this church."[7]

Third, Luke wasn't afraid to show the early Christians as they really were—warts and all. Yes, they were an alive, loving, generous people, and, yes, there were people like Barnabas in their midst. But they had their "bad apples," too, and Luke was candid enough to tell about them as well. This community of faith wasn't perfect, by any means, but it would do its best to protect its integrity.

THE APOSTLES DEFY THE AUTHORITIES AND PROCLAIM JESUS (5:12-42)

When our children were small, my wife and I bought them a clown punching bag. This life-sized vinyl clown was weighted at the bottom, so that every time one of my children would hit, kick, or tackle him, he would pop right back up. No matter how they abused him, he would always return to a vertical position, smile firmly in place. He was the epitome of the phrase, "You can't keep a good man down."

As Luke comes to the end of his first section of Acts about the early Christians gathering a community, he hits upon the theme of resiliency one more time. The apostles preached about Jesus, but they were arrested and threatened by the Jewish authorities. They escaped prison and started to preach again. Again, the authorities threatened them. But no matter how many times they were knocked down, those early believers kept getting back up. Finally, one of the Pharisees named Gamaliel spoke a word that carried the day: We will leave these men alone. If this movement is bogus, it will fail. If it is of God, we won't be able to squash it no matter how hard we try.

The religious leaders agreed it was a good plan. They called in the apostles, flogged them, ordered them

Gamaliel

His name means "recompense of God." He was the grandson of the great teacher Hillel, the founder of one of two leading scribal schools of thought (Shammai was the founder of the other influential school). His son Simon was a leader of the revolt against Rome (Josephus, *J. W.* 4.159). Toward the end of the first century, his grandson, Gamaliel II, was the "prince" (*Nasi*) of the reorganized, post-revolt, Sanhedrin. This information allows modern readers to appreciate the stature of this man and to understand why Luke could portray him as having such influence over the Sanhedrin.

not to utter another word about this Jesus, and let them go. But they must have known, even as they said it, that they were wasting their breath. Chapter 5 ends with this telling line: "And every day in the temple and at home, they did not cease to teach and proclaim Jesus as the Messiah" (Acts 5:42). That clown simply would not stay down. Luke wants us to know that this is a community that can't be threatened into submission.

CONCLUSION

By the time we get to the end of chapter 5, the community has been gathered. Luke has shown us how they were formed, who their leaders were, how they were empowered by God's Spirit, and what they did. By the end of chapter 5, this learning, worshiping, celebrating, awestruck, generous, and contagious band of ordinary men and women had started to turn their world upside down. They had reached thousands of people with the good news of Jesus Christ, but they still had issues to address. Most notably, they had to decide how inclusive they would be. Is this way of Jesus for Jews only, or is it for the world? In the next section of Acts, Luke shows us how those early believers answered that question and how they moved out into their world to break down walls.

NOTES

[1] Curtis Vaughan, *Acts: A Study Guide* (Grand Rapids MI: Zondervan, 1974), 23.

[2] Quoted in William H. Willimon, *Acts*, Interpretation Commentary (Atlanta: John Knox Press, 1988), 34.

[3] Ibid.

[4] Quoted in "Dumbed Down" by Timothy Renick, *The Christian Century*, September 2007, 27.

[5] Ibid.

[6] Calvin Miller, *A View from the Fields* (Nashville: Broadman, 1978), 20–21.

[7] Stanley Hauerwas and William H. Willimon, *Resident Aliens* (Nashville: Abingdon, 1989), 132.

QUESTIONS FOR REFLECTION AND DISCUSSION

(1) How do you relate the miraculous events at Pentecost to your own experience with God? How do you explain the wind, fire, and speaking in tongues? Do you ever long for miracles from God?

(2) When you read about the marks of the first Christian community, what emotions do you feel? Do you think the modern church has the six characteristics of the first church?

(3) Do you agree that our culture has so stressed the personal dimension of faith that it has neglected the communal dimension?

(4) How do you explain the strange story of Ananias and Sapphira? What does the story say to modern readers?

(5) Have you ever suffered because of your faith in Christ? What do you think made those early believers so tenacious and resilient?

BREAKING DOWN WALLS (ACTS 6–15)

Focal Text—Acts 15:6-11

After the Christian community was gathered, it had significant issues to address and formidable walls to demolish. Primarily, the church had to answer the question, "Who should receive the gospel?" If it was only for Jews, that would be easy. They could just keep the gospel "in house" and reach out to their own kind. But if the gospel was for the world, that complicated things. That meant there were many walls to break down, many stereotypes to debunk, and many prejudices to overcome.

In chapter 6–15 of Acts, Luke sets out to show us how the church did that. He moves through a series of "wall toppling" incidents and then culminates this section of Acts with the Jerusalem Council, where the early church leaders gathered to make an official statement about the universality of the gospel.

We will move quickly through these incidents, noticing how the early Christians broke down those walls, and then focus on Peter's address at the Jerusalem Council in Acts 15:6-11. His words there capture the essence of this entire section of Acts.

SEVEN DEACONS ARE SELECTED (6:1-7)

In his first example of wall breaking, Luke describes the church's choosing seven men to be deacons. This one episode shows the early church breaking down several significant walls.

The problem in the church was that some of the "Hellenistic" (Greek) widows were being neglected when food was distributed. Frankly, those women were probably used to being neglected because they simply didn't have many of the "coins" of human worth. They were widows in a male-dominated culture. They were poor in a culture that valued wealth. And they spoke Greek in a

The Seven

The seven are the men chosen to "serve tables." Yet there is no record that they do any such thing. Only two of the seven are treated in any detail, Stephen (chs. 6–7) and Philip (ch. 8; 21:8-9). It is difficult to distinguish sharply between the activities of these two representatives of "the seven" and the actions of "the Twelve": both groups work wonders and preach. *Historically*, "the seven" were perhaps not merely a group appointed by the Twelve to "serve tables"; rather, they served as the *leaders* of the Hellenist Christians, with "the Twelve" serving as the leaders of the "Hebrew" Christians. The Hellenists looked to *seven* leaders since "local officials of the Jewish culture that primarily spoke Aramaic. In dealing with these Hellenistic widows,

community and also ancient councils consisted of seven members" (Conzelmann, 45).

Luke, attempting to offer a simplified and unified portrayal of the early church, relegated "the seven" to a less significant role. Still, the traditions he inherited reveal perhaps that this group of seven played a more significant role in the early Jerusalem church. Regarding other members of the seven, later church tradition said that Prochorus became an associate of the Apostle John and Nicanor founded the heretical Nicolaitans of Rev 2:6.

Hans Conzelmann, *Acts of the Apostles,* Hermeneia (Philadelphia: Fortress, 1987).

culture that primarily spoke Aramaic. In dealing with these Hellenistic widows, the early believers had to surmount a gender wall, an economic wall, and a language wall. If the Christian community would be attentive to poor widows who didn't even speak the common language, it would be attentive to anyone. And, Luke tells us, the believers removed all of those walls and made sure the women got their food. Seven men were selected to serve those women, to ensure that the church would be the one place where they would not be forgotten.

STEPHEN IS ARRESTED, SPEAKS TO THE COUNCIL, AND IS STONED (6:8–8:3)

One of those seven deacons was Stephen, whom Luke tells us was "full of grace and power" and "did great signs and wonders among the people" (Acts 6:8). But Stephen was so winsome and persuasive that he also attracted the attention of the religious authorities—who were not at all pleased with his message. They captured him and hauled him before the synagogue council.

There Stephen delivered the longest speech recorded in the book of Acts. The speech "lurches from selective reminiscence to passionate indictment."[1] Stephen spoke about the history of the Jewish people, focusing primarily on their rejection of God and God's prophets before hammering home his point: "You stiff-necked people, uncircumcised in heart and ears, you are forever opposing the Holy Spirit, just as your ancestors used to do" (Acts 7:51).

The Martyrdom of Saint Stephen

Both Annibale Carracci and his less famous nephew and student Antonio Carracci produced artistic interpretations of the martyrdom of Stephen. The painting depicts Stephen being stoned outside the city (Acts 7:58). Being cast outside the city may serve to make Stephen's death more like that of Christ, who was executed outside the city as well. Stephen is depicted praying that the Lord receive his spirit and for his perse-cutors (Acts 7:59-60). The viewer

Annibale Carracci (1560–1609). *The Stoning of Saint Stephen*. Louvre, Paris, France. (Credit: Erich Lessing / Art Resource, NY)

of the painting, like Stephen, is allowed to see "heavens opened and the Son of Man standing at the right hand of God" (Acts 7:56). The angel descending to receive Stephen is not a specific feature of the text of Acts. The man sitting on the right, guarding the clothes of Stephen's attackers, is clearly Paul (Saul). Is he reaching out imploring Stephen's killers to stop, foreshadowing his eventual repen-tance? Or does he want to participate?

It was a message guaranteed to raise the ire of his listeners: "They became enraged and ground their teeth at Stephen" (Acts 7:54). Then they dragged him out of the city and stoned him to death, making Stephen the first Christian martyr (or, at least, the first *recorded* Christian martyr).

As a tantalizing hint of things to come, Luke ends the episode about Stephen with this footnote: "the witnesses laid their coats at the feet of a young man named Saul" (Acts 7:58). This Saul "approved of their killing him" (Acts 8:1) and became a leader in the movement to stamp out Christianity. He entered house after house and hauled both men and women to prison.

PHILIP, PETER, AND JOHN GO TO SAMARIA (8:4-40)

Luke will return to this Saul shortly and, in fact, make him the lead character in his story, but next he turns to Philip, like Stephen one of the seven deacons chosen by the church, "who went down to Samaria and proclaimed the Messiah to them" (Acts 8:5). Here was another mammoth wall that was demolished. In New Testament times, the Jews thought of the Samaritans as religious and racial half-breeds and refused to associate with them. In going to preach the gospel in Samaria, Philip was toppling a huge racial wall. That someone from the Christian community would go anywhere outside the Jewish circle was surprising; that someone from the Christian community would go to Samaria was unbelievable! Eventually Peter and John joined Philip there to fortify the Christian witness to the Samaritans (see page 91, **Map of Palestine in New Testament Times**).

Luke mentions two specific people touched by Philip's ministry in Samaria. He first mentions Simon, a magician who was so impressed with the kind of power Philip possessed that he offered Peter money for it. He wanted this power, but he wanted it for all the wrong reasons. Simon wanted it so he could be popular and famous, and Peter blasted him for his distorted thinking and unscrupulous motives. The power of the Holy Spirit is not for sale, and it is not for personal aggrandizement. The power of the Holy Spirit is for creating a kingdom of love and servanthood where hungry widows and despised Samaritans are welcomed.

The other person Philip deeply affected was an Ethiopian eunuch. This court official of Candace, the Ethiopian queen, was riding along in his chariot, reading aloud the 53rd chapter of Isaiah. When Philip heard what he was reading, he asked him if he knew what it meant. The eunuch confessed he needed someone to explain the passage to him. Philip was happy to oblige and to tell the man the fulfillment of that passage had come in Jesus. The man

Simony

Simon's attempt to purchase the power to bestow the Holy Spirit gave rise to the term "Simony" to denote the purchase or sale of spiritual things. It was consistently condemned in various church councils (such as Chalcedon [5th c.] and Trent [16th c.]) and the writings of influential church thinkers, such as Aquinas [13th c.]). Such regular official denunciations actually serve as evidence that the practice was widespread, for one generally does not exert energy condemning something that does not exist.

Ethiopia

Ancient Ethiopia is not identical to the modern country by this name. Ancient Ethiopia is the same as the nation of Cush in the Old Testament (Gen 10:6-8) and was located in area of modern Sudan. The civilization of Cush lasted until c. AD 350. The culture was a source of fascination to the ancients. Pliny the Elder (*Nat.* VI.186–92) speaks of reports that certain regions of Ethiopia produced human monstrosities: people without noses, upper lips, or tongues. Some tribes were said to follow a dog as their king, while others followed a one-eyed king. Awareness of these popular stereotypes of Ethiopians makes God's directing of Philip to invite an Ethiopian into the fold of God's people especially provocative. This gospel really is for all types of people! Other relevant biblical texts are Isa 11:11 and Zeph 3:10.

believed, the chariot was stopped, and an impromptu baptism took place in a local river.

Talk about the gospel going universal! First the Hellenistic widows. Then the hated Samaritans. Then this exotic official from a foreign land. This message of Jesus was for everyone.

SAUL OF TARSUS IS CONVERTED ON THE ROAD TO DAMASCUS (9:1-31)

Astonishingly, the message of Jesus was even for that fire-breathing, church-hating Pharisee named Saul. The good news of the gospel was powerful enough to reach him and change his life. Paul's Damascus

Philip Baptizing Ethiopian Eunuch

Alexandre-Denis Abel de Pujol (1787–1861). *St. Philip baptising the Queen of Ethiopia's eunuch on the road from Jerusalem to Gaza*. 1848. Oil on canvas. (Credit: Réunion des Musées Nationaux / Art Resource, NY)

Road conversion was so significant to the Christian movement that it is recounted three times in Acts—here in Luke's voice and twice again in Paul's voice (22:3-16; 26:4-23).

The events in that conversion experience are familiar to nearly anyone who has read the Bible. Paul's miraculous conversion has become common knowledge—the light from heaven, the voice from on high, the blindness that came upon him, the visit from a man named Ananias who restored Paul's sight and baptized him, and then Paul's burning desire to take Jesus to the world.

What is often overlooked in his conversion experience is this line from God about the reason for Paul's conversion: "I myself will show him how much he must suffer for the sake of my name" (Acts 9:16). Paul wasn't converted so he could get more glory, power, or success. He was converted so he could suffer for the name.

I mentioned earlier that I have often prayed for a Damascus Road experience, a time when God would come out in the open and bowl me over with bright lights, loud words, and absolute certainty. After reading Acts for this study, I'm not so sure I knew what I was praying. I realize now that none of us should pray for a Damascus Road experience unless we can also bear to hear God say, "I want to show you how much you will have to suffer."

One more thing should be noted with regard to Damascus Road experiences: They come at God's discretion. Paul's miraculous conversion experience did not come to him because he deserved it or had prayed for it. It came only because God chose to give it to him. Saul of Tarsus was an angry legalist determined to destroy Christians, and, out of the blue, he got a dramatic encounter with God.

Some people get those life-changing encounters, though they seem to be few and far between. Others yearn for them but don't get them and have to be content with hints and hunches. God is the giver of all kinds of conversions, though, and we learn to be grateful for whatever experiences God chooses to give us.

The Conversion on the Road to Damascus

Though inspired by the Carracci family (see [The Martyrdom of Saint Stephen]), Michelangelo is generally credited with the creation of the Baroque style. To be noted is his realism and use of light. The light almost beats down on Saul as he lies on the Damascus road, offering a sense of the overwhelming power of the light that has blinded him. The outstretched arms communicate a desperate reaching out for help. The man with him, cowering behind the horse, is in no position to help Saul. Saul's help must come from the Lord.

Michelangelo Merisi da Caravaggio (1573–1610). *The Conversion of Saint Paul.* S. Maria del Popolo, Rome, Italy. (Credit: Scala / Art Resource, NY)

PETER PERFORMS MIRACLES, VISITS CORNELIUS, AND PREACHES TO THE GENTILES (9:32–11:18)

After telling about Saul's dramatic conversion, Luke abruptly shifts the spotlight back to Simon Peter. In the rest of chapter 9, all of chapter 10, and part of chapter 11, we see more walls crumbling as Peter realizes the gospel is not just for "insiders" (the Jews) but also for "outsiders" (the Gentiles).

We learn first, though, of two miracles Peter performed. In Lydda, Peter healed a man named Aeneas, who had been bedridden and paralyzed for eight years. Peter healed him, and "all the residents of Lydda and Sharon saw him and turned to the Lord" (Acts 9:35). Then Peter went to Joppa and did something even more astounding. He raised from the dead a widow named Tabitha ("Dorcas" in Greek). Again, people were amazed and "many believed in the Lord" (Acts 9:42).

Luke explains nothing about these healings and raising-from-the-dead stories. How God's agent, Peter, was able to bring healing and new life perhaps can't really be explained. The story can only be told and marveled at. But one thing is for certain: there was a power at work that was available even to sick

Miracle Stories

In the New Testament, miracle stories follow a form or pattern common to miracle stories across cultures and time. The miracle story describes a condition of need that ordinary means cannot address. The sick (or even dead!) person and the miracle worker encounter each other. The miracle worker does or says something that results in a (usually instantaneous) cure, accompanied by some confirmation, including the amazement of any onlookers. As with other features of biblical narrative, worldviews and assumptions of readers will shape their judgments regarding the historicity of miracles. Throughout church history, even before the Age of Reason and the Enlightenment, the allegorical and/or typological interpretation of miracle stories—as well as the rest of the Bible—was not uncommon. The Reformers tended to favor a literal approach, both with respect to miracle stories and other biblical texts.

Harold E. Remus, "Miracle: New Testament," *ABD* 4.856–69.

Tanner

Because tanners, by necessity, worked with dead animals, they were chronically unclean. The Mishnah compares the tanner's uncleanness to that of persons afflicted with boils or polyps or who collected dogs' excrement. Some rabbis even required tanners and others who lived in such uncleanness to "put away their wives"; that is, they did not require women to remain married to such men (see *m. Ket.* 7.10). For readers who know this, Peter's residing with "Simon the Tanner" ironically sets up the following scene where Peter appears so scrupulous about matters of ritual cleanness. Peter's residence may also foreshadow his eventual association with another group of "unclean people," the Gentiles.

paralytics and dead widows, the same power that had come in the wind and fire at Pentecost.

Luke ends those episodes with the comment that "Peter stayed in Joppa for some time with a certain Simon, the tanner" (Acts 9:43). That sets the stage for the next adventure Peter would have and the next wall that would topple. In Joppa, Peter had his own conversion experience, as he discovered that Gentiles are to be included in "the Jesus Way." His encounter with Cornelius was a turning point in his understanding of God's plan and the church's mission.

The events in Peter's transformation can be summarized like this: Cornelius, a Gentile Roman army officer, has a dream telling him to seek out a certain Simon, who is called Peter. Meanwhile, Peter is having a dream of his own. In Peter's dream, he is commanded to eat unclean animals, which he finds repulsive. But a voice in the dream cautions Peter not to call unclean what God has deemed clean.

Unclean Animals

The Old Testament lays out in summary fashion the categories of clean and unclean animals in Lev 11 and Deut 14. Curious to modern readers is the whole notion of dividing the world into things clean and unclean. Anthropologists have noted that across human cultures all people are inclined to organize and categorize their worlds into spheres of clean and unclean. Hence, "the clean/unclean distinction is Israel's symbolic means of structuring the world. Clean animals stay in their own sphere (land, water, air) and move in a way appropriate to that sphere (walking, swimming, flying). Unclean animals cross between the spheres and use inappropriate locomotion" (Watts, 167; see [Purity]). Though moderns tend not to "divide up" the world as did Jews in the first century, even modern people have a sense of "clean" and "unclean." For example, there are foods that modern Westerners tend not to eat: road kill and domesticated, in-home animals (pets). They would consider this "gross," or "unclean." And moderns certainly know what "dirty words" are and even have appropriate rites to "cleanse" the mouth: washing it out with soap.

J. W. Watts, "Leviticus," *MCB* 157–74.

Peter is summoned to Cornelius's house and arrives to discover a roomful of Gentiles. The meaning of his dream becomes clear to him. He is not to think of these Gentiles as unclean people but as people loved by God. He preaches a sermon, and the Holy Spirit comes upon the Gentiles just as it had come upon the Jews at Pentecost.

What you realize when you come to the end of this episode is that Peter has had a conversion experience of his own. Paul had one, but Peter had one too. Anthony Robinson and Robert Wall, in their book *Called to Be Church*, write,

Conversion is often understood as conversion from no faith to faith, or from one faith to another. Furthermore, conversion is just as often understood to be something that happens just once in a person's life. Peter's experience throws a monkey wrench into those assumptions: as a follower of Jesus, he is converted to a new understanding of the church's faith and mission, one that leads him to step across boundaries and barriers that had, up to this point, seemed impenetrable. Not only as a believer and follower of Christ, but also as an apostle and leader of the church, Peter finds his mind opened and his life redirected. Conversion continues.[2]

Peter's conversion is a reminder to us that we have a mission field *inside* the church, as well as *outside* the church. It also reminds us that our own personal conversion is still very much in process.

PAUL AND BARNABAS GO TO ANTIOCH TO MINISTER FOR A YEAR (11:19-30)

It is easy to get the impression that the events in Acts happened rapidly. We have the idea, for example, that when Paul was on his missionary journeys, he would stop in one place for a week to two, then be off to another place for a week or two, hopping hurriedly from one pagan city to the next. In truth, he often stayed months, and even years, in those places. The events in the book of Acts took thirty years to unfold, so things weren't moving as rapidly as they seem.

When Barnabas went to Antioch to proclaim the message of Jesus, he found a most responsive crowd, and many made commitments of faith. The field was so ripe for the harvest that he invited Saul, soon to be known as Paul, to join him. Paul went to Antioch too. Luke says, "So it was for an entire year they met with the church and taught a great many people, and it was in Antioch that the disciples were first called 'Christians'" (Acts 11:26). For an entire year, Barnabas and Paul ministered in this large city of 800,000 people, and the gospel gained a foothold. Eventually, Antioch, from this simple beginning, would become the preeminent church in the ancient world, supplanting Jerusalem as the capital of Christianity.

Antioch

 This city was the capital of the Roman province of Syria (see page 92, **Map of Paul's First Missionary Journey**). It was founded by Seleucus Nicator c. 300 BC, who named the city after his father. The city may represent an ancient example of "urban sprawl," for it was actually a combination of four cities that eventually grew into one another during the first 125 years of Antioch's existence. Estimates of the population of the city in the first century AD range from 500,000 to 800,000 (Jerusalem, by comparison, is estimated to have had a population of between 25,000 and 50,000). The Jewish historian Josephus stated that Antioch was third among cities of the Roman world, ranking only behind Rome and Alexandria. Antioch was made a free city by Pompey in 64 BC.

F. J. Foakes Jackson and Kirsopp Lake, *The Beginnings of Christianity: The Acts of the Apostles*, 5 vols. (Grand Rapids MI: Baker, 1979), 4.127–28; T. C. Smith, "Antioch," *MDB* 34–35.

Antioch on the Orontes.
(Credit: Library of Congress, LC-matpc-02183/ LifeintheHolyLand.com)

PETER IS MIRACULOUSLY DELIVERED FROM PRISON (12:1-25)

Acts 12 is a long parenthesis. When chapter 11 closes, Paul and Barnabas are in Antioch preaching the word. When chapter 12 closes, Luke reports, "Then after completing their mission Barnabas and Saul returned to Jerusalem and brought with them John, whose other name was Mark" (Acts 12:25). In between those two verses, Luke squeezes in a lot of action completely unrelated to what Barnabas and Paul were doing in Antioch:

• King Herod kills James, the brother of John, and imprisons Peter.
• Peter is delivered from prison by an angel.
• Peter escapes prison and goes to be with the other disciples but, in a scene of comic relief, can't get in the door because of a flustered maid named Rhoda.
• Herod is enraged and gets struck down by God.

In spite of mad kings and rampant persecution, the church continued on its way. As Luke puts it, "But the word of God continued to advance and gain adherents" (Acts 12:24). Those early believers, in spite of strong opposition, kept proclaiming the good news of Jesus . . . and breaking down walls every chance they got.

PAUL AND BARNABAS SET SAIL AND SHARE THE GOOD NEWS (13:1–14:28)

Chapters 13 and 14 of Acts describe Paul's first missionary journey (see page 92, **Map of Paul's First Missionary Journey**). Perhaps the best way to capture the events in these two chapters is to underscore the highlights of this trip:

- The journey lasted about two years, from AD 47–49. The chapters read rapidly, but the events unfolded slowly.

> **King Herod**
>
> The Herod of Acts 12 was more commonly referred to as Agrippa I. He was a grandson of Herod the Great. Agrippa was friends with Emperor Caligula, who became the Roman emperor in AD 37 and appointed Agrippa I ruler of the territory located northeast of Galilee and formerly ruled by one of Herod the Great's sons. When Agrippa's uncle, Herod Antipas (the Herod of Luke's Passion Narrative), was deposed in AD 39, Agrippa was given the regions that he had ruled, Galilee and Perea. In AD 41 Agrippa became the ruler of Samaria, Judea, and Idumea as well. He now ruled territory as extensive as that of Herod the Great. He died in Caesarea in AD 44.
>
> R. O. Byrd, "Agrippa I and II," *MDB* 16.

- At the beginning of the journey, Luke writes of "Barnabas and Saul," as if Barnabas were the leader. Very quickly, though, the order is reversed and we read about "Paul and Barnabas." Perhaps it speaks volumes about Barnabas, the encourager, that he was willing to defer to Paul's leadership.
- John Mark began the journey with Paul and Barnabas but left when they reached Perga and returned to Jerusalem. There has been much speculation about John Mark's departure, and Luke never spells out why he left. We do know, though, that Paul was not happy with him and refused to let him go on the next journey (see Acts 15:38).
- Along the way, Paul and Barnabas encountered a magician on the island of Cyprus, Paul preached a sermon in Antioch of Pisidia that led to persecution, Paul healed a cripple in Lystra and was stoned, and Paul and Barnabas started at least four churches—in Pisidian Antioch, Iconium, Lystra, and Derbe.
- Paul and Barnabas had a consistent method on the journey—(1) they chose the great centers of population, the cities of influence, in which to plant the gospel; (2) they sought out a synagogue and preached first to the Jews and then let the message spread from there; and (3) they took great care to preserve the fruit of their work by encouragement, instruction, and organization.[3]

St. Paul's Church

The church actually belongs to a much later period (c. 4th century). Tradition has it that the church was built over the site of the synagogue where Paul preached. The official archaeological report of the University of Michigan was open to the possibility: "Who shall say that this building may not stand upon the site of the synagogue where Paul and Barnabas preached (Acts XIII)?"

George W. Swain, "Archaeological Results of First Importance Attained by the Near East Research of the University of Michigan During Its First Campaign," 19 August 1924, Francis W. Kelsey papers, box 73, p. 4, Kelsey Museum Collection, Bentley Historical Library, University of Michigan, Ann Arbor MI. Report can also be found online: http://ella.slis.indiana.edu/~zestrada/Antioch/Articles%20and%20Reports.html (5 July 2006).

Church of St. Paul, Pisidian Antioch (Credit: Todd Bolen, "Church of St. Paul," [cited 17 September 2007]. Online: http://www.bibleplaces.com.)

After their two-year journey, Paul and Barnabas sailed back to Antioch. Luke says, "When they arrived, they called the church together and related all that God had done with them, and how he had opened a door of faith for the Gentiles" (Acts 14:27). A door of faith for the Gentiles? The *Gentiles,* of all people? The Jews had always seen themselves as God's chosen people. And now the doors were being thrown open to the *Gentiles?*

That issue was enough to warrant an extended conversation. And that's exactly what happened. Paul and Barnabas headed to Jerusalem to discuss the issue with the apostles and elders there. The Jerusalem Council, as it has come to be called, was convened for the purpose of hashing out this thorny question: "Just *who* is the good news of Jesus Christ *for,* anyway?" This council—and in particular Peter's speech before the council—will be the focal point of this section of our study.

THE JERUSALEM COUNCIL DECIDES TO WELCOME GENTILE CHRISTIANS (15:1-41)

Some of us cringe when we start reading Acts 15. As we read about those early Christians heading toward Jerusalem to discuss the Gentile question, we're reminded of some of the infamous "called business meetings" we've attended.

We remember how our fervor took a drastic nosedive after the church called a special session to ponder a particular issue.

Maybe we were enthused about a new ministry we'd gotten involved in to help the homeless in our community. Or maybe we were hopeful about an innovative way to reach out to teenagers. Whatever it was, we were excited about this new thing God was getting ready to do . . . until the church got hold of it in a business meeting.

"Who's going to assume liability in this ministry to the street people?" someone snarled from the back of the room. And a bitter dispute started to take shape.

"Our church has never done anything like that with teenagers before," someone cautioned. And the line was drawn in the sand.

Eventually, our fervor faded as the rhetoric intensified. We decided to give up the ministry idea because it was too divisive.

That easily could have happened in Acts 15. Wonderful things had been happening in the early church. Paul and Barnabas had just returned from a most successful voyage to faraway places. People in those places had been receptive to the gospel, churches had been established, and the good news of Jesus was spreading around the world. Things were going great . . . but then there came the ominous "called business meeting."

It was called because certain people had concerns about opening a door of faith to the Gentiles. Those critics were willing to accept the Gentiles as long as the men among them were willing to be circumcised: "Unless you are circumcised according to the custom of Moses, you cannot be saved" (Acts 15:1). In other words, you Gentiles can be Christians as long as you become covenant Jews too.

The debate was large enough that it demanded a broader venue. Paul and Barnabas headed to Jerusalem to discuss the issue, and the Jerusalem Council was convened. Amazingly, this potentially divisive "called business meeting" turned out to be a model of how to deal with conflict in the church. Instead of becoming divisive and hurting the church, it addressed the Gentile issue head-on and energized the church. By the conclusion of the Jerusalem Council, the thorny Gentile issue had been addressed and a resolution had been agreed upon. The Gentiles were welcomed into the Christian fold. God had been working in their hearts, so why not acknowledge and celebrate it?

Circumcision

The history of this ceremony among the ancient Israelites is shrouded in mystery. Scholarly consensus connects the pivotal story of Gen 17 with the priestly source of the exilic period, which may indicate that by this time the ceremony had emerged as a most significant feature of Jewish religion. This story portrays circumcision as the mark of being a member of the covenant people. Jewish texts composed during the Maccabean period (c. 160s BC), such as Jubilees and 1 Maccabees, communicate the depth of commitment among pious Jews to be faithful to the law and tradition that required males belonging to God's people to be circumcised (see in the Apocrypha 1 Macc 1:54-64 for a good illustrative text of the importance of being circumcised and keeping the law of Moses within the Jewish community).

John B. Polhill, "Circumcision," *MDB* 156–57.

Perhaps the key to the Jerusalem Council was the brief but powerful speech Peter gave to the leaders in Jerusalem (Acts 15:6-11). It was a model of brevity, but it must have made a huge impact on the council. Actually, to say it was a speech is overstating the case; Luke gives us only four sentences that Peter spoke. But those four sentences packed quite a wallop.

Peter laid out his argument for including the Gentiles in three simple points:

(1) God chose me to deliver the good news to the Gentiles. (Acts 15:7)
(2) God honored my words by drawing the Gentiles to him. They received the Holy Spirit just as we did. (Acts 15:8-9)
(3) Why shouldn't we celebrate what God has done among them? Why would we want to burden the Gentiles with rules and regulation we ourselves have been unable to bear? (Acts 15:10-11)

That concise three-point sermon carried the day. Once Paul and Barnabas echoed Peter's words, the outcome was certain. The walls had come down. James simply acknowledged what everyone saw was true: the gospel of Jesus was for Gentiles as well as Jews.

It is easy for us today to read Acts 15 and fail to see what a dramatic thing happened there. It is easy for us to read Peter's words about receiving the Gentiles and fail to realize how revolutionary they are. All their lives, people like Peter and Paul had been living with walls. Ancient Jewish religion was full of walls that were taken for granted by anyone who grew up in that religious system. Nowhere is that more evident than in the design of the Jewish temple, the magnificent edifice in Jerusalem that served as the centerpiece of Jewish religion. When we remember the symbolism in the design of the temple, we see just how remarkable Peter's brief speech was (see page 95, **The Jerusalem Temple**).

As you approached the temple in Jerusalem, you would come first to the Court of the Gentiles. This was as far as any non-Jew could go. There was a wall erected that prevented any Gentile from going closer to the Holy of Holies, the center altar that housed the symbolic presence of God. So there was a *social wall* in the temple that blocked entry to Gentiles. They could gather in the Court of the Gentiles, but that was as far as they could go.

Next you would come to the Court of Women. This was a court where the Jewish women could congregate, but there was a wall there too, and beyond that wall the women could not go. So there was a *sexual wall* in the temple as well. All of the women of that day knew there was an unwritten sign posted on that wall: "Beware! No women can proceed beyond this point."

If you continued your tour of the temple, you would next come to the Court of Israel. This was the place for the Jewish men who wanted to worship God at the temple. They gathered in the Court of Israel, but this was as far as they could go. There was a wall there that prohibited the men from getting any closer to the Holy of Holies. Only priests could go beyond this point, and the laymen knew it. There was a *sacral wall* that separated the laity from the clergy.

Then there was the Court of Priests. This was the gathering place for the priests of Israel, but even the priests faced a wall. On beyond the Court of Priests was the Holy of Holies, and only one person, the high priest, on one day, the Day of Atonement, could enter the Holy of Holies. Even the priests were "walled out." There was a *spiritual wall* in the temple that prohibited even the ordained from getting close to God.

That was the system Peter knew. He had grown up, as a good Jew, instinctively knowing the pecking order. The symbol of his religion, the temple, revealed it clearly. There was a social barrier that excluded the Gentiles. There was a sexual barrier that excluded women. There was a sacral barrier that excluded laypeople. And there was, finally, a spiritual barrier that excluded even the priests. The whole system was filled with walls!

William Hull, in his book *Beyond the Barriers,* discusses these walls in the temple architecture and concludes,

These walls . . . were not merely decorative but were determinative of Israel's basic understanding of the nature of religion. They did not serve to simply organize available space in convenient fashion; instead, they literally put each person in his or her proper place in relation both to others and to God. In so doing, they confirmed and reinforced assumptions which were operative wherever the Jewish religion was practiced throughout the world.[4]

So, when Peter stood up at the Jerusalem Council and said what he said, it was almost a miracle. Certainly, his speech was counter to everything he had learned growing up and counter to everything his culture still held to be true. What he was saying, incredibly, was that the old system wasn't valid anymore. The walls—in particular the wall blocking the Gentiles—had come down.

When you think about what has happened in this section of Acts (chs. 6–15), you see how Luke methodically has shown the early church removing those walls. When the church selected seven deacons to take care of non-Jewish women, it was breaking down walls. When Philip, Peter, and John went to Samaria to preach the gospel, they were breaking down walls. When the church accepted an angry Pharisee named Saul, it was breaking down walls. When Peter visited Cornelius and preached to the Gentiles, he was breaking down walls. And when Paul and Barnabas sailed to foreign cities to declare the good news, they were breaking down walls too. This entire section of Acts tells the story of a series of walls being demolished by the early believers in Jesus.

CONCLUSION

After describing the Jerusalem Council, Luke gives a brief account of a dispute that occurred between Paul and Barnabas. Barnabas wanted to take John Mark on the next missionary journey, but Paul had been burned once by John Mark and didn't want to try him again. Paul and Barnabas decided to part ways. Barnabas took John Mark with him and sailed away to Cyprus. Paul chose Silas to accompany him, and off "they went through Syria and Cilicia, strengthening the churches" (Acts 15:41).

The community has been gathered. The walls have been broken down. Now the priority of the early church is taking the gospel to the ends of the earth. In the next section of Acts, chapters 16–20, Luke shows us the church spreading the word.

NOTES

[1] William H. Willimon, *Acts,* Interpretation Commentary (Atlanta: John Knox Press, 1988), 62.

[2] Anthony B. Robinson and Robert W. Wall, *Called to Be Church* (Grand Rapids MI: William B. Eerdmans, 2006), 158.

[3] Curtis Vaughan, *Acts: A Study Guide* (Grand Rapids MI: Zondervan, 1974), 102.

[4] William E. Hull, *Beyond the Barriers* (Nashville: Broadman, 1981), 27.

QUESTIONS FOR REFLECTION AND DISCUSSION

(1) Do you long for a Damascus Road experience like the Apostle Paul had? Do you ever wish God would be more visible and dramatic in your life?

(2) What walls still exist in our society? What should we, as the church, be doing to break down those walls?

(3) Does the modern church do a good job of handling internal conflict? What can we learn from Acts 15 about dealing with thorny issues in the church?

(4) What does Peter's speech at the Jerusalem Council teach us about handling conflict? About being persuasive? About leadership?

(5) Are there some walls in your own relationships that need to come down? Are there people or groups of people with whom you need to reconcile?

SPREADING THE WORD (ACTS 16–20)

Focal Text—Acts 20:17-35

When the curtain goes up for the third act in the Acts drama, it's as if Luke, the director of the play, decides to get out his telescopic lens and do "close-ups" of one actor. From chapter 16 to the end of the story, Paul becomes the focal point. We occasionally glimpse Silas or Timothy in the background, but the camera is trained primarily on Paul. Chapters 16, 17, and 18 give details about Paul's second missionary journey. Chapters 19 and 20 tell us about his third missionary journey.

We know there were other Christians out there spreading the word, telling their friends and neighbors this incredible story about Jesus. We know, for example, that Barnabas and Mark took off to Cyprus to tell the good news there. But, for Luke's purposes, Paul is the preeminent example of one spreading the word, so Luke will focus on him the rest of the way in Acts.

PAUL AND SILAS HEAD TO MACEDONIA AND ARE IMPRISONED (16:1-40)

In chapter 16, Paul is on the move (see page 93, **Map of Paul's Second Missionary Journey**). He is working in Derbe and Lystra, where he enlists Timothy to join him on the trip. He is working in Troas, where he has a vision telling him to go to Macedonia. And he is working in the Macedonian city of Philippi, where several significant things happen.

In Derbe and Lystra (16:1-5), Paul recruited Timothy to join him on the journey. Since Timothy's father was Greek, Paul had Timothy circumcised to validate his "Jewishness." Without this circumcision, Timothy would not have been permitted to preach in the Jewish synagogue. Paul also delivered the decrees of the Jerusalem council to the churches around Derbe and Lystra,

Philippi

Originally named Krenides, the city was renamed Philippi by Philip II, father of Alexander the Great, c. 358 BC. The city was brought under Roman rule in 168 BC. Inscriptions reveal a very religiously pluralistic city. In 42 BC, Philippi was the location of a key battle in which the forces of Antony and Octavian (Augustus) defeated the Republican forces. At that time, Octavian made the city a Roman colony. In 31 BC, when Octavian defeated Antony, Octavian renamed the colony *Colonia Julia Augusta Victrix Philippensis*, adding *Augusta* to its name. The city became a popular place for Roman veterans to retire. As a Roman colony, Philippi had the right of autonomous government, did not have to pay tribute to Rome, and its citizens had the right of private ownership of property.

Richard A. Spencer, "Philippi," *EDB* 1048–49; T. C. Smith, "Philippi," *MDB* 683–84.

telling them the good news that the walls had been broken down and that Gentiles were welcome in the church. This message was evidently received with joy, and the churches were strengthened in the faith and increased in numbers daily.

Then Paul moved on to Troas (16:6-10). After the Spirit had forbidden him to preach in Asia and Bithynia, he went to Troas and had a vision telling him to come to Macedonia. So Paul and his entourage—which now included Silas, Timothy, and Luke—took off for Macedonia, "being convinced that God had called us to proclaim the good news to them" (16:10). Then Paul went into Macedonia and settled in the city of Philippi (16:11-40). Luke records four significant events that happened at Philippi.

First, a woman named Lydia became Paul's first convert in Macedonia. Her conversion, unlike Paul's, was quiet and unspectacular. She listened intently to Paul and opened her heart to his message. She and her household were baptized, and then Lydia opened her home to Paul and his traveling companions.

Second, Paul delivered a young slave woman from her "spirit of divination." She was making her owners a great deal of money by her fortune telling, Luke says, and they were not pleased when Paul removed the spirit from her. When her owners saw what Paul had done, they realized immediately that their fortune-telling business was history. They seized Paul and Silas, dragged them to the authorities, and fabricated charges against them. Paul and Silas were flogged and tossed into jail.

Third, a Philippian jailer came to faith in Christ. While Paul and Silas were in prison, an earthquake shook the place so hard all the doors were opened and everyone's chains were unfastened. The jailer, assuming that the prisoners would escape, drew his sword and was about to kill himself. Paul shouted in a loud

Baptism of Households

Acts 16:31-33 (cf. 16:14–15) speaks of whole households being baptized. Christians who view baptism as a personal and individual response of faith to the gospel might be troubled by statements that seem to indicate that the whole household can be saved based solely on the response of the head of that household (cf. 16:14b–15a, 31). To be sure, v. 32 makes clear that Paul and Silas spoke the word of the Lord to all who were in the jailer's house, allowing for the conclusion that baptism only followed personal confession.

While one likely can assume that confession of some sort preceded baptism, modern readers still must not assume that individualistic notions of personality and identity prevailed in the ancient world. Ancients had a more collectivist understanding of personality and identity. That is, persons in antiquity tended to find their identity and personality in the context of the larger significant groups in which persons were embedded. The most significant such group would be the kinship group, and especially the immediate household of which one was a part. Members of the household would likely take their "cues" even of *voluntary* religious identification from the head of the household, which was usually male (cf. 16:31–33), but could also be female (cf. 16:14–15). Texts within the gospel tradition do indicate, however, that the gospel message could divide families (see Matt 10:34-39 || Luke 12:51-53; 14:26; Matt 19:29 || Mark 10:29; cf. Matt 12:46-50 || Mark 3:31-35 || Luke 8:19-21).

Bruce J. Malina, *The New Testament World: Insights from Cultural Anthropology*, 3rd ed. (Louisville KY: Westminster/John Knox Press, 2001), chs. 2 and 5.

---

voice, telling the jailer not to hurt himself, for all the prisoners were still in place. The jailer, trembling, asked Paul and Silas, "Sirs, what must I do to be saved?" (16:30). It is likely that, given the context of the question, he was not speaking theologically at all. He simply wanted to know how he could escape all of this chaos and consternation! But they answered, "Believe on the Lord Jesus, and you will be saved, you and your household" (16:31). The man and his family were baptized without delay, and the jailer then took Paul and Silas into his home, washed their wounds, and fed them. Like Lydia, his conversion was confirmed by his hospitality.

Fourth, Paul and Silas were released from prison. We don't know the reasons, but the next morning the magistrates sent the police to free Paul and Silas. Did the mysterious earthquake have anything to do with their sudden release? Had it dawned upon the magistrates that Paul and Silas had never had a trial? We don't

Prison Conditions

Based on descriptions of ancient prisons found in the literature of antiquity, Charles Talbert offers a vivid description that allows one to imagine the setting:

Prison was the most severe form of custody. Jailers were notorious for their cruelty. . . . The inner prison was the worst possible site. . . . Many would be confined in a small area; the air would be bad; the darkness would be profound; the stench would be almost unbearable.

Charles Talbert, *Reading Acts: A Literary and Theological Commentary of the Acts of the Apostles* (New York: Crossroad, 1997), 154.

know the answers to those questions; we just know that Paul and Silas were set free. Paul, however, was pointed in his response to the magistrates: "They have beaten us in public, uncondemned, men who are Roman citizens, and have thrown us into prison; and now are they going to discharge us in secret? Certainly not! Let them come and take us out themselves" (16:37). The magistrates, afraid now because of what they had done to Roman citizens, came and apologized and asked them kindly to leave the city. Paul and Silas returned to Lydia's home for a while, received some needed words of comfort, and left Philippi.

This chapter provides us not only a snapshot of Paul, but also a snapshot of the way the early church spread the word about Jesus. In this one chapter, we see some of the distinctive trademarks of the first community of Christians, what Robinson and Wall call "resurrection practices."[1] Five trademarks are evident in Acts 16: (1) hospitality (shown by Lydia and the jailer), (2) economic justice, (3) suffering, (4) worship and prayer, and (5) teaching and learning.

Take those five trademarks of the early church, and you see how the first believers chose to spread the word about Jesus. How did those Christians spread the word? They practiced hospitality. They demonstrated economic justice. They suffered courageously. They worshiped and prayed. They taught and learned. And people outside the church took notice and came to faith in Christ.

PAUL CAUSES AN UPROAR IN THESSALONICA AND BEREA AND PREACHES IN ATHENS (17:1-33)

In Acts 17, Luke tells us about three cities Paul visited after he was released from jail in Philippi.

Thessalonica. In Thessalonica, Paul ventured to the synagogue to reason with people. Several of the Jews were persuaded and became Christians. But there was a faction in the city that was not pleased with what Paul and Silas were doing. Luke says they "became jealous, and with the help of some ruffians in the marketplace, they formed a mob and set the city in an uproar" (Acts 17:5).

This mob stormed the house of a man named Jason, who must have been housing Paul and Silas. When the ruffians couldn't find Paul and Silas, they dragged poor Jason before the city authorities, made him post bail, and finally let him go. The believers in Thessalonica, sensing that Paul and Silas were in

Thessalonica

The city was founded in 316 BC, transferred into Roman hands in 168 BC, and made a free city within the Roman Empire in 42 BC. Because the city was both a port city and located along a major road, the *Via Egnatia*, trade and commerce were central to the city's importance. The city was quite diverse religiously in Paul's time. Mystery religions, the worship of Egyptian deities, and Emperor worship were quite prominent. According to the narrative of Acts, there was also a synagogue in the city.

Richard S. Ascough, "Thessalonica," *EDB* 1300–1301.

Thessalonica. (Credit: Todd Bolen, "Thessalonica from north," [cited 20 September 2007]. Online: http://www.bibleplaces.com.)

great jeopardy, sent them off to Berea under cover of darkness.

Berea. The people in Berea received Paul and Silas with open arms. Luke says, "The Jews were more receptive than those in Thessalonica, for they welcomed the message very eagerly and examined the scriptures every day to see whether these things were so" (Acts 17:11).

But when the ruffians in Thessalonica heard that Paul and Silas were being welcomed in Berea, they traveled there themselves (a journey of about fifty miles) and stirred up the crowds. What looked like revival quickly degenerated into criticism and chaos. Once again, the believers came to the rescue, and the Berean Christians snuck Paul out of town. They escorted him to Athens, while Silas and Timothy remained behind in Berea.

Athens. While Paul waited in Athens for Silas and Timothy to join him, he took stock of the city and was distressed to see that it was full of idols. He went

Athens

Athens reached its zenith in the late fifth century BC, with great building programs, the construction of the Parthenon, and, over time, the establishment of significant schools of Greek philosophy. This legacy continued into Paul's time. The city had the reputation of being religious, curious, and learned—all stereotypical traits that the narrative of Acts alludes to and employs.

to the synagogue and spoke of Jesus, and he ventured out into the marketplace and spoke of Jesus there too. In the marketplace, he spoke to the Epicureans, who worshiped pleasure, and the Stoics, who worshiped reason, declaring to them the good news of Jesus and his resurrection.

He was eventually escorted to the Areopagus, an aristocratic council of

The Agora of Athens

Mars Hill is the hill situated just below the Acropolis (loc. 10). One can see that Paul's encounter with the philosophers took place under the imposing presence of the Acropolis. The Royal Stoa (loc. 2) is the likely spot where readers can imagine Paul's speech before the Areopagus to have taken place.

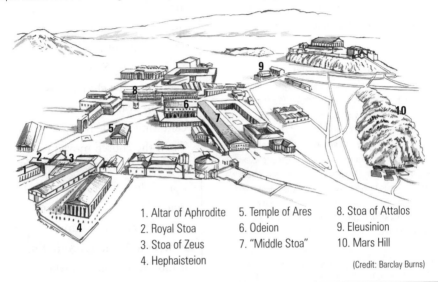

1. Altar of Aphrodite	5. Temple of Ares	8. Stoa of Attalos
2. Royal Stoa	6. Odeion	9. Eleusinion
3. Stoa of Zeus	7. "Middle Stoa"	10. Mars Hill
4. Hephaisteion		

(Credit: Barclay Burns)

intellectual Athenians, where he was given opportunity to explain his strange teachings. Willimon writes, "We have seen the power of the gospel to reach rich and poor, Jew and gentile, slave and free, male and female. But can the gospel hold its own in the sophisticated intellectual environment of a university town?"[2]

Paul gave it his best shot and laid out a reasoned defense of his beliefs, and the Athenians responded to Paul's sermon in several ways. Some scoffed, especially about his talk of resurrection. Some procrastinated and said they'd hear him again. And a few took a leap of faith and decided to become believers. Two converts—Dionysius and Damaris—are mentioned by name.

When we read about Paul's experience in Athens we realize that much of it is instructive for us today and provides good "teaching points" for this study.

For one thing, we realize that, like the people of Athens, people in our day are attracted only to "the new and improved." Acts 17:21 could be the motto for contemporary American culture: all the people "spend their time in nothing but telling or hearing something new."

For another thing, Paul's experience in Athens reminds us that people are still enamored with spirituality. Paul's comment to the Athenians in Acts 17:22 is

Athenian Curiosity

The Athenian propensity to talk about or listen to new things, about which Luke comments in 17:12, was proverbial in Luke's world. A most colorful description of Athenian curiosity is found in the Chariton's ancient novel, *Chaereas and Callirhoe*:

> When they were all alone they debated where to sail to. One of them said: "Athens is nearby. . . ." And they all liked the idea of making for Athens. But Theron did not like the inquisitive ways of the town. "Look, are you the only people who don't know what busybodies they are in Athens? They're a nation of gossips, and they love lawsuits. There'll be hundreds of nosey parkers in the harbor wanting to know who we are and where we got this cargo we're carrying. Nasty suspicions will seize hold of the malicious minds—and it's the Areopagus straightway, in Athens, and magistrates who are more severe than tyrants.

B. P. Reardon, ed. and trans., *Collected Ancient Greek Novels* (Berkeley: University of California Press, 1989), 33.

also appropriate for our society: "I see how extremely religious you are in every way." Americans are definitely religious. I like the quote attributed to Richard Halverson, former chaplain of the United States Senate: "In the beginning the church was a fellowship of men and women centering on the living Christ. Then the church moved to Greece, where it became a philosophy. Then it moved to Rome, where it became an institution. Next, it moved to Europe, where it became a culture. And, finally, it moved to America, where it became an enterprise."[3] In a culture where religion has become an enterprise and church has become big business, how do we stay true to the gospel?

Third, Paul-in-Athens reminds us that we are supposed to go to the marketplace. Give Paul credit: he got out there nose to nose with the intellectuals of his day and told the story of Jesus. He didn't linger at the church; he ventured to the marketplace where the unbelievers were. When we think about our own discipleship, we realize how often our faith is limited to the church. Many of us have spent far more time in committee meetings at church than we have sharing our faith in the marketplace. Many of us know far more people at church than we know in the marketplace. Paul-in-Athens indicts our introverted Christianity.

Finally, Paul's experience in Athens reminds us that faithfulness supersedes success. After Paul's address before the Areopagus, some scoffed, some procrastinated, and some believed. But Paul's harvest wasn't particularly plentiful. Dionysius and Damaris and a few others professed Christ, but that was it. Paul had done what he needed to do, though. He had told his story and delivered the truth. He had been faithful in spreading the word.

PAUL TRAVELS TO VARIOUS CITIES PREACHING THE GOSPEL (18:1-28)

"After this Paul left Athens and went to Corinth" (Acts 18:1). Talk about taking the gospel to the marketplace! Corinth was as secular and sinful a place as there was in the ancient world. The Greeks had the phrase "to play the Corinthian," which meant to live a life of lustful debauchery. Corinth was notorious for its drunkenness and dishonesty, so to take the gospel there was no small undertaking. Paul went and stayed perhaps two years, though, spreading the word among people immersed in a sinful culture.

Luke tells us several things about Paul's work in Corinth and then, at the end of chapter 18, in other places:

• He meets Aquila and his wife, Priscilla, who share his tentmaking craft. Aquila and Priscilla are Christian Jews from Rome who had moved to Corinth. They receive Paul with open arms and invite him to stay with them and work with them.

Corinth

The Corinth of Paul's day served as the capital of the Roman province of Achaea, a status it had held since 27 BC. The city was economically significant, as well. Its strategic location allowed the city to serve as a bridge connecting mainland Greece and the Peloponnesian Peninsula, as well as to two major seas, the Aegean and Adrian. Two ports, Cenchreae and Lechaeum, situated to the east and west, respectively, kept commerce and travelers moving in and out of Corinth.

(Credit: Jim Pitts)

Religiously, the city was quite diverse. Older Greek religions experienced something of a revival, including the worship of Apollo, Aphrodite, Poseidon, Asclepius, and Demeter. Non-Greek religions, such as those honoring the Egyptian deities of Isis and Serapis and the Phrygian goddess Cybele, and Judaism were also prominent in Corinth. Paul's lengthy discussions regarding the issue of Christian participation in pagan rituals and cultic practices (see 1 Corinthians 8–10) speaks to the deep-seated cultural currents that could affect believers in Corinth.

Wendell Willis, "Corinth," *EDB* 279–81.

- Silas and Timothy arrive from Macedonia to help Paul, but even with their help, Paul finds ministry to the Jewish community in Corinth to be dismal and discouraging. He shakes the dust from his clothes and announces that, from this time forward, his primary ministry will be to Gentiles, not Jews. Then, in typical Pauline fashion, he sets up his new headquarters right next to the Jewish synagogue. He will now declare the gospel from the house of Titius Justus, a Christian who just happens to live adjacent to the place where the Jews come to worship.

- Paul receives a vision from the Lord telling him not to be afraid, to be bold in his witness, and to know that there are many other believers in Corinth.

- Paul comes under attack again. The Jews in Corinth drag him before Gallio, the local ruler, and accuse him of inventing a religion that is contrary to the law. Gallio will hear none of it, however, and declares the matter to be a local religious dispute and not something a government official should adjudicate. In other words, he sees Paul's Christianity not as a threatening new religion but as a variation of Judaism. The Jews are incensed at this and express their hostility by beating up Sosthenes, the leader of the synagogue.

- Paul then completes his second missionary journey. He sails across the Aegean Sea to Ephesus, then from Ephesus across the Mediterranean Sea to Caesarea. From Caesarea, he goes to Jerusalem and then to Antioch, and his journey is complete. In Acts 18:22, the second journey ends. He stays in Antioch for a short time before heading out again to spread the word on his third journey (see page 94, **Map of Paul's Third Missionary Journey**).

- Luke adds a final word about another missionary who is spreading the word. His name is Apollos, and he evidently has a lot going for him. He is eloquent, well versed in Scripture, enthusiastic, a fine teacher, and bold in his witness. But Luke says he knew only the baptism of John. He hadn't heard all the details about Jesus and the miraculous events at Pentecost, so Priscilla and Aquila "took him aside and explained the Way of God to him more accurately" (Acts 18:26). It is interesting to note that Luke now mentions Priscilla first as Apollos's tutor. It is obvious that Apollos is being taught the basics of the Way by a woman, which seems to indicate that Paul's advice on women remaining silent and not teaching men (1 Tim 2:12) was not applicable for all churches.

At the end of chapter 18, the word about Jesus is still being spread to the world. Paul has completed his second missionary journey and is launching his third, and Apollos has been schooled in the Way so that he can be a missionary too. Apollos goes to Achaia where he joins the chorus of those "showing by the scriptures that the Messiah is Jesus" (Acts 18:28).

Apollos

What one learns from the portrayal of Apollos in Acts 18 corresponds well with what Paul says of him in 1 Corinthians. For example, Acts indicates that Apollos went to Corinth after Paul established a community there (18:27). Paul describes himself as one who plants and Apollos as one who watered (1 Cor 3:6), as though Apollos followed the apostle (cf. 1 Cor 3:10).

Acts makes reference to the eloquence of Apollos (18:24). While Paul never explicitly contrasts himself with Apollos on matters of rhetorical eloquence, Paul does imply, with some defensiveness, a certain *lack* of eloquence on his part (cf. 1 Cor 1:18-25; 2:1-5), as though he knew that he was being criticized for such (cf. 2 Cor 10:10). Paul also was aware of some divided loyalties at Corinth, which included some rivalry between followers of Apollos and Paul (1 Cor 1:12). Further, Paul felt compelled to give special attention to his relationship with Apollos as fellow ministers to the Corinthians (1 Cor 3:5-15; 4:6-7). This all *might* imply that the supporters of Apollos were attracted to his skills of eloquence in speech and interpretation, especially as compared to Paul's lack of the same.

PAUL PREACHES IN EPHESUS AND ENRAGES THE FOLLOWERS OF ARTEMIS (19:1-41)

The action in Acts 19 is fast and furious—Paul preaching in Ephesus and infuriating the followers of the goddess Artemis—but, once again, the events actually occurred over a long period of time. Paul was in Ephesus for perhaps three years, so this one chapter deals with an extended time.

We know from some of Paul's other letters that the stay in Ephesus was filled with controversy and struggle. In the Corinthian letters we learn that Paul suffered greatly in Ephesus, and there is even a suggestion in 1 Corinthians 15:32 that he was thrown into a beast-filled arena but escaped unharmed. In his letter to the Romans, we learn that Paul was imprisoned in Ephesus with two men named Andronicus and Junia. When you think of Paul in Ephesus, think trouble, conflict, and discouragement.

Luke had to be selective about what he would include regarding Paul's stay in Ephesus, and he condensed the action down to four incidents. Why Luke included these four and omitted others is beyond us, but we do know that he chose to focus on these four incidents in Ephesus:

Ephesus

 In Paul's day, the city of Ephesus was over 900 years old and had experienced, as any city of that age, quite a history. It had been ruled by the Persians, Alexander and his various successors, and rulers of the region of Pergamum, until moving under Roman control in 133 BC. From that time it served as the official residence of the governor of the Roman province of Asia.

Ephesus was among a select group of cities during the Roman imperial period to have the honor to build temples dedicated to patron deities. The patron deity of Ephesus was Artemis.

According to Acts, Paul was instrumental in founding the Christian community at Ephesus (18:19), though his coworkers, particularly Priscilla and Aquila, made significant foundational contributions (18:26). Paul's extended stay of some three years (19:10, 22; 20:31) speaks to the importance of the city in the Pauline mission.

David E. Aune, "Ephesus," *EDB* 413–15.

---

(1) In Acts 19:1-7, he tells us about Paul guiding some Ephesians from "the baptism of John" to "the baptism of Jesus." These people knew of John the Baptist and his way and had chosen to follow it. But they had not heard about Jesus and his way. They knew the way of repentance and works, of putting your hand to the plow and being faithful. But they knew nothing of grace and celebration, of receiving God's Spirit and dancing through life. So Paul told them about the way of Jesus, and they came to know the joyful way of grace.

That is still a necessary movement in the church. Even today, many faithful Christians know the way of John the Baptist. They know of repentance and works, but they have not yet found the incredible freedom that can be theirs in Jesus. Karl Olsson, in his book *Come to the Party*, wrote, "It is apparent that there are two kinds of people in the church: those who bring gifts to God in order to secure his blessing and those who adore him because they are already secure in his blessing."[4]

There are unblessed Christians, stuck in the way of John the Baptist, trying to earn God's love and win God's blessing. And there are blessed Christians, frolicking in the way of Jesus, grateful for God's love and secure in God's blessing. Paul wanted to move the Ephesians into the "blessed" category.

(2) In Acts 19:8-10, Luke tells of Paul's discouragement with his Jewish kinsmen. For three months, Paul went to the Ephesian synagogue and "argued persuasively about the kingdom of God" (Acts 19:8). That was Paul's custom on his journeys. He would begin at the synagogue and tell his kinsmen that the Messiah had arrived in the person of Jesus of Nazareth. But, more often than not, his preaching fell on deaf, even hostile ears. Remember, at Corinth he had

become frustrated with the Jews and shunned the synagogue, making his preaching headquarters in the house of Titus Justus. Here, in Ephesus, Paul's frustration boils over again. Paul storms out of the synagogue and makes his headquarters in the lecture hall of a man named Tyrannus. For two years, Paul preached from the lecture hall "so that all the residents of Asia, both Jews and Greeks, heard the word of the Lord" (Acts 19:10). From whatever pulpit he could find, Paul would be faithful in spreading the word.

(3) In Acts 19:11-20, Luke once again addresses the subject of magic. As he did in chapter 8 in telling about Simon Magus, he affirms again that the name of Jesus is not to be used flippantly and for personal gain. Jesus is not a talisman for people who want to do tricks.

The way Luke tells the story, Paul had become so powerful that God could do extraordinary miracles through him. Even his handkerchiefs and aprons had healing power. Some itinerant Jewish exorcists noticed this incredible power and decided they wanted some of that action themselves. Luke's version of the story is a not-so-subtle example of New Testament humor. The Jewish exorcists try casting out an evil spirit in the name of Jesus, but the evil spirit

Followers of John the Baptist

Biblical testimony makes clear that John the Baptist had his own circle of disciples (Matt 9:14; 11:2 || Luke 7:18; Luke 11:1; John 1:35; 4:1). And testimony from texts such as Acts 18:25 and 19:3 indicate that John's message of baptism reached out into the larger Greco-Roman world.

The Gospels seem concerned to make clear that John is subordinate to Jesus (see such texts as Matt 3:14 and John 1:8, 20; 3:30). In fact, many believe that one of the major points of the Lukan birth narrative, as he offers his narrative of Jesus' and John's respective annunciations and births, is to show Jesus to be superior to John. Attention to such a concern on the part of New Testament writers offers indirect evidence that followers of the Baptist continued to offer some competition to the Jesus movement at the time these narratives were composed. The story of Paul and followers of John in Acts 19 is one such story that serves to show that, properly understood, John's purpose is to *prepare* the way for Jesus.

J. Bradley Chance, "John the Baptist," *MDB* 458–59.

Magical Incantation

Given the pervasiveness of magic in the ancient world, it is not surprising that archaeologists have recovered a number of magical formulae. Among various magical papyri is one dating to c. AD 300 that offers the following formula for exorcism. Note among the names a variation on the name Jesus:

> Standing opposite, adjure him. The adjuration is this: "I adjure thee by the god of the Hebrews Jesu, Jaba, Jae, Abraoth, Aia, Thoth, Ele, Elo, Aeo, Eu, Jiibaech, Abarmas, Jabarau, Abelbel, Lona, Abra, Maroia.

C. K. Barrett, ed., *The New Testament Background: Writings from Ancient Greece and the Roman Empire That Illuminate Christian Origins*, rev. ed. (New York: HarperSanFrancisco, 1989), 34.

rises up to say, "Jesus I know, and Paul I know; but who are you?" (Acts 19:15). Then the man with the evil spirit leaps upon them, overpowers them, and sends them running naked and wounded down the road. "When this became known to all residents of Ephesus, both Jews and Greeks, everyone was awestruck" (Acts 19:7).

The way of Jesus is not for charlatans and magicians. His power is available only to people like Paul, people who suffer and sacrifice for the name. And those who were practicing magic, Luke says, burned their expensive books (worth fifty thousand coins) and became believers.

(4) The final vignette from Paul's stay in Ephesus is in Acts 19:21-41. It concerns a riot that broke out because of Paul's preaching. Luke, in his typically understated way, simply writes, "About that time no little disturbance broke out concerning the Way" (Acts 19:23).

The riot was about economic self-interest, pure and simple. The silver-smiths who fashioned trinkets in honor of the goddess Artemis saw Paul as a threat. If people started believing this message about Jesus, Artemis would lose supporters and their trinket business would take a nosedive. So, a silversmith named Demetrius led a movement to silence Paul—and preserve his own profits!

Ephesus was filled with confusion, Luke says, and two innocent traveling companions of Paul, Gaius and Artistarchus, were dragged into the theatre. Paul wanted to go into the crowd himself but was prevented by some of the other believers. Eventually, the town clerk of Ephesus tried to restore order by reminding the people that, of course, the city was known for its worship of the great goddess, Artemis. But the Christians had neither robbed the temple nor blasphemed her name and weren't really guilty of any crime. Besides, the one thing the Roman Empire would not abide was a riot in one of its cities, and this scene was perilously close to becoming just that. The town clerk dismissed the assembly, and the Christians escaped harm by the skin of their teeth.

Luke must have included that vignette for a good reason: he wanted to remind his readers that the way of Jesus is always corrupted when economic self-interest enters the picture. You cannot serve God and money.

Artemis

Artemis of Ephesus was the local manifestation of a truly cosmopolitan deity in the Greco-Roman world. In fact, she was the most widely followed deity in Paul's day. She was closely associated, particularly among the Ephesians, with fertility and the protection of new life. A statue of Artemis from Ephesus shows numerous eggs or breasts protruding from her torso—symbols of fertility. Ancient inscriptions indicate that devotees looked to her for answered prayer and the offering of salvation, including liberation from fate and demonic forces.

Twice each year the city of Ephesus would sponsor civic celebrations that revolved around the city's devotion to the goddess. Involved in the celebration was the procession of the images of Artemis from the Artemisium, the temple of Artemis, through the city streets. The temple that stood in Paul's day dates back to the fourth century BC and was considered one of the seven wonders of the ancient world. The civic celebrations brought many pilgrims to Ephesus, and the "tourist industry" was the primary means of economic support to the city.

Statue of Artemis. Ephesus Archaeological Museum, Ephesus, Turkey. (Credit: Vanni / Art Resource, NY)

Joseph A. Coray, "Artemis," *EDB* 107.

PAUL PREACHES IN VARIOUS CITIES AND MEETS WITH THE EPHESIAN ELDERS (20:1-38)

When I took my Bible down to the Alsea River there in Oregon and started reading Acts, I expected several things to happen. I expected to learn new truths about the book. I expected to refresh my memory about the key events in the life of Paul. I expected to be puzzled by some of the strange happenings in the early church. And I expected to have my own commitment challenged and energized. All of those things happened, and I profited greatly by reading Acts.

I did not expect to laugh. I had no idea I would find myself chuckling as I read Luke's account of the early church. After all, this is the inspired word of God, serious stuff, a chronicle of great import. Who knew that Acts would be so laced with humor that I would chuckle all the way through it?

But I did. I would be reading along, caught up in the serious proceedings of the book when, all of a sudden, Luke would surprise me with a funny tale that would make me smile, if not laugh out loud.

There was staunchly orthodox Simon Peter having naughty dreams about unclean animals and having his life changed by these "profane" visions.

There were Paul and Barnabas singing hymns in a prison cell.

There was Paul refusing to leave the jail in Philippi until the authorities came to him and apologized for the way they had treated him.

There was Paul storming in protest out of the synagogue in Corinth and then, in typical Pauline in-your-face style, opening up shop in the house right next door.

There was that indomitable spirit who overpowered the exorcists in Ephesus and said, "Jesus I know, and Paul I know; but who are you?" (Acts 19:15).

And then there was this episode in Acts 20 where Paul's sermon was so long (and boring?) that a young man named Eutychus fell asleep and toppled out of a third-story window.

Is it possible we miss Luke's levity simply because we assume the Bible is supposed to be somber and serious? After reading Acts again, I'm convinced Luke had a fine sense of humor.

After the uproar in Ephesus with the followers of Artemis (in chapter 19), Paul left for Macedonia. He stayed in Greece for three months and was about to sail for Syria when he received word of a plot to take his life. He decided to return to Macedonia and was accompanied on that trip by seven representatives (bodyguards?) from some of the churches he had previously visited. The group eventually made it safely to Troas where the infamous incident with Eutychus took place.

Since Paul was planning to leave Troas the next day, he had to say all he was going to say in that one sermon. Luke says he continued speaking until midnight. Poor Eutychus "began to sink off into a deep sleep" (Acts 20:9) and then fell out the window. Paul and the others present hurried to check on him and Paul reassured everyone, "Do not be alarmed, for his life is in him" (Acts 20:10). Whether Paul performed a miracle and raised the boy or was just announcing that the boy wasn't dead after all is not clear. What is clear is that Eutychus was alive and well, and those in the house "were not a little comforted" (Acts 20:12).

After the Eutychus incident, we get a blow-by-blow account of the places Paul visited next. This is another of those "we passages" where Luke must have been along on the journey. "*We* went ahead to the ship and set sail for Assos"

Miletus

The city where Paul offered his farewell address to the Ephesian elders was a significant seaport city and commercial center, having four harbors and three market areas. One of the agoras is pictured below on the left. Due to silt deposits over the centuries, modern Miletus (Palatia) is now five miles inland. Two symbols of the cosmopolitan character of the city were its theater and public bath, the ruins of the latter pictured below on the right.

The Agora at Miletus. (Credit: Todd Bolen, "Miletus in the Bible," [cited 17 September 2007]. Online: http://www.bibleplaces.com.)

The Bathhouse at Miletus. (Credit: Todd Bolen, "Roman Bathhouse," [cited 17 September 2007]. Online: http://www.bibleplaces.com.)

(Acts 20:13), he wrote. Then it was on to Mitylene, Chios, Samos, and Miletus, as Luke ticked off the names of the places he himself was visiting with Paul.

It was while in Miletus that Paul sent a message to the elders of the church at Ephesus that he would like to visit with them. The elders made the thirty-mile journey to Miletus, and Paul delivered then the only sermon in the book of Acts addressed to Christians. All of Paul's other speeches and sermons were addressed to Jewish or Gentile unbelievers, but the message to the elders was directed to leaders of the church. Since Luke was with Paul at this time, he probably heard the sermon firsthand and recalled it when he wrote Acts years later. Paul's message to the Ephesian elders in Acts 20:17-35 is the focal text for this third section of Acts.

The address to the Ephesian elders is Paul's "farewell address." Throughout the Bible, biblical heroes give farewell addresses that have great significance. Jacob (Gen 49), Joseph (Gen 50), Moses (Deut 32), and Joshua (Josh 23) all give farewell addresses in the Old Testament. But Paul's farewell discourse most resembles the one Jesus gives in John 13–17. Willimon writes, "The parallels between Jesus' farewell speech to his disciples and Paul's farewell speech to the Ephesian elders are too numerous to be coincidental."[5] Vaughn comments that

---

Paul's Farewell Speech and the Pauline Epistles

Ben Witherington notes that the content and vocabulary of this address, the only one in Acts in which Paul addresses a Christian audience, offer many connections with the Pauline corpus. He lays out the data and offers a helpful discussion of the issues (610–11). Some of the more important similar features are summarized below:

Vocabulary/concept	Reference in Acts	Reference in Pauline letters (indisputably authentic only)
Summarizing work as "serving the Lord"	20:19	Rom 1:1; 12:11; Phil 2:22
Jewish persecution	20:19	2 Cor 11:24, 26; 1 Thess 2:14-16
Teaching from house to house	20:20	Rom 16:5; Philem 21
Preaching to both Jews and Gentiles	20:21	Rom 1:16; 1 Cor 9:20
Faith in the Lord Jesus	20:21	Rom 10:9-13
Uncertainty about Paul's future	20:22	Rom 15:30-32
Willing to surrender his own life for the gospel	20:24	2 Cor 4:7–5:10; 6:4-10; Phil 1:19-26; 2:17; 3:8
Preaching the gospel of the grace of God	20:24	Gal 1:15-16; 2 Cor 6:1

Ben Witherington III, *The Acts of the Apostles: A Socio-Rhetorical Commentary* (Grand Rapids MI: Eerdmans, 1998).

Paul's farewell address is "the most personal and most affectionate address which has come down to us from Paul."[6]

In his farewell address in Acts 20:17-35, Paul does two things. First, he describes and affirms his own ministry, and, second, he challenges the Ephesian elders to pick up the torch and adopt this style of ministry themselves. In other words, the farewell address is not only Paul's attempt to explain his own approach to ministry; it is also his call for others to give it a try. We do well to focus a moment on this farewell address to remember what a call to ministry involves and what a life of ministry looks like.

Perhaps the best way to understand Paul's concept of ministry in his farewell address is to remember the biblical idea of "covenant." Theological ethicist William May has written that biblical covenants typically have four distinguishing characteristics:

(1) A person receives a primal gift or costly sacrifice that both marks and changes a life.

(2) In response to this gift, a person makes promises and accepts obligations.

(3) As a person lives within the context of the gift and the promises, fidelity becomes the norm. The person is determined to be true to the covenant.

(4) There are occasions and events that enable a person to renew the covenant and pass it on to others.[7]

We can take those four ideas and overlay them on Acts 20:17-35 to get a better understanding of Paul's concept of ministry. Paul and the Ephesian elders (and you and I and any person who would be a Christian leader) are to make the following declarations:

First, I will live in response to the gift. Paul knew that his ministry was a response of love to what God had done for him. He spoke to the Ephesian elders about "the ministry I received from the Lord Jesus, to testify to the good news of God's grace" (Acts 20:24). His ministry was a gift, something he had received from the Lord Jesus. Freely Paul had received, and freely he would give. Later he encouraged the Ephesian elders to "shepherd the church of God that he obtained with the blood of his own Son" (Acts 20:28). The church itself was God's initiative, inaugurated by the blood of Jesus and empowered by the Holy Spirit. Paul's ministry and the churches he served were all gifts of God.

Paul's ministry covenant began, then, with the recognition that God had sought him, forgiven him, called him, and empowered him. Paul's impetus for ministry can be summed up by the words of John, "We love because he first loved us" (1 John 4:9). We minister because he first loved us. We preach because he first loved us. We attend church business meetings because he first loved us. We endure difficult people because he first loved us. Ministry begins with the gift of God's love.

According to Paul, Christian leaders have received their ministry as a gift from the Lord Jesus, and their calling is to testify to the good news of God's grace. Freely we have received that grace, and freely we give it to others.

Second, I will make promises that give direction and courage to my ministry. After receiving the gift of God's grace, Paul made some promises that shaped his ministry, promises that also fortified him when the going got tough. He told the Ephesian elders, "I do not count my life of any value to myself, if only I may finish my course and the ministry I received from the Lord Jesus . . ." (Acts 20:24). God had gifted Paul, and Paul, in response, had determined to value his ministry more than his happiness or satisfaction. Come what may, he was going to finish his course and accomplish his ministry. In short, Paul had promises to keep.

The Whole Purpose of God

AΩ The Greek word translated "purpose" is *boulē*, often rendered by such other English words as *intention, plan,* or *decision.* In the Lukan writings, the term, when used in reference to the *boulē* of God, can best be rendered as "plan" or "purpose," depending on the context. The line between the two renderings, however, is quite thin, for God's plans are in accordance with God's purposes and God's purposes eventuate in God's plans. Luke

Johnson summarizes the Lukan use of the phrase as follows: "The 'will of God' (*boulê tou theou*) is a favorite term of Luke's, denoting God's plan for history (see Acts 2:23; 4:28; 13:36; 20:27). Contrasted to it is the 'will of man' in Acts 5:38" (123).

Luke Timothy Johnson, *The Gospel of Luke* (SacPag 3; Collegeville MN: Liturgical Press, 1991).

Those promises enabled Paul "not to shrink" when confronted by the challenges of his ministry. Twice in his farewell address he used that phrase. In Acts 20:20 he says, "I did not shrink from doing anything helpful, proclaiming the message to you and teaching you publicly and from house to house . . . ." Then in Acts 20:27 he says, "I did not shrink from declaring to you the whole purpose of God . . . ." Paul wasn't going to shrink from his tasks because of the covenant he had made with God. He had made some promises, and he was going to be true to them.

Third, I will be motivated by fidelity, not success. Once the gift has been received and the promises made, we embark upon a long journey of being faithful to the call. Most of Paul's farewell address speaks to this third point—his fidelity to his call.

He reminds the Ephesian elders how he "served the Lord with humility and tears, enduring the trials that came to me through the plots of the Jews" (Acts 20:19). He reminds them how he went from house to house sharing the gospel with both Jews and Greeks. He tells them that he coveted no one's silver, gold, or clothing while he was among them but worked with his own hands to support himself and his companions. He tells them he tried to be an example of one who supports the weak and lives by the philosophy that it is more blessed to give than to receive. What Paul really does in his farewell address is remind those Ephesian elders that he had been one of them for three years. They had heard him "talk the talk." But they had also seen him "walk the walk."

Fourth, I will renew my covenant and pass it along to others. Paul had received the gift, made some promises in response to that gift, and then lived in fidelity to the covenant. But in his farewell address he renewed that covenant and then challenged the Ephesian elders to make covenants of their own. The farewell address served two purposes. It enabled Paul to stoke his own coals, to remember his promises and adventures, and to gain strength from them. But it also stirred the Ephesian leaders to be faithful to their own ministry covenants. There is definitely a passing of the baton in the passage as Paul senses that his own ministry is drawing to a close.

Paul's premonition was right on target. From this time on, he spends most of his days in a prison cell. The next section of Acts (chs. 21–28) focuses on Paul taking a stand for Christ in prison. He will take no more missionary journeys and establish no more churches. His witness will take a different form, and people like the Ephesian elders will have to spread the word out there in the world.

Chapter 20 ends on a sad note. Paul prays for these Ephesian friends, and "there was much weeping among them all; they embraced Paul and kissed him, grieving especially because of what he had said, that they would not see him again" (Acts 20:37-38). But Paul had been able to reaffirm his own covenant with God and encourage his friends to do the same.

As Paul trudges toward a ship bound for other places, I can't help thinking of something the painter Vincent Van Gogh once said:

> There may be a great fire in your soul, yet no one ever comes to warm himself at it, and the passersby only see a wisp of smoke coming through the chimney, and go along their way. Look here, what must be done? Must one tend the inner fire, have salt in one-self, wait patiently yet with how much impatience for the hour when somebody will come and sit down—maybe to stay? Let him who believes in God wait for the hour that will come sooner or later.[8]

Amid all the sadness in Paul's departure from his Ephesian friends, there was joy too. At least he had been able to share his great inner fire. At least there had been some who would come along and sit with him and be warmed by his passion.

CONCLUSION

At the end of Acts 20, Paul is getting on a ship heading for Jerusalem. He has spent several years sailing around his part of the world, establishing and strengthening churches, facing stiff opposition, and generally being the cantankerous, confident person who has inspired generations of Christians.

Most of the rest of Acts deals with Paul in prison. He will be paraded before a succession of powerful people, but not once will we get the idea that Paul is intimidated. He will continue to be cantankerous and confident as he takes his stand for Christ before these government officials.

Luke has shown us the first Christians *gathering a community*. He has given us specific examples of those believers *breaking down walls*. He has followed Paul on his missionary journeys and shown us the church *spreading the word*. Now he will take us behind prison bars to show us that, even there, the church is *taking a stand*.

NOTES

1 Anthony B. Robinson and Robert W. Wall, *Called to Be Church* (Grand Rapids MI: William B. Eerdmans, 2006), 203–210.

2 William H. Willimon, *Acts*, Interpretation Commentary (Atlanta: John Knox Press, 1988), 142.

3 Quoted in James B. Twitchell, *Shopping for God* (New York: Simon & Schuster, 2007), 20.

4 Karl Olsson, *Come to the Party* (Waco: Word Books, 1972), 80–81.

5 Willimon, *Acts*, 156.

6 Curtis Vaughan, *Acts: A Study Guide* (Grand Rapids MI: Zondervan, 1974), 131.

7 For further treatment of the characteristics of biblical covenants, see Robinson and Wall, *Called to Be Church*, 237–45.

8 Vincent van Gogh, *The Complete Letters of Vincent van Gogh*, vol. 1 (Greenwich CT: The New York Graphic Society, 1959), 197.

QUESTIONS FOR REFLECTION AND DISCUSSION

(1) This session mentions five trademarks of the church in Acts 16: hospitality, economic justice, suffering, worship and prayer, and teaching and learning. Are those still trademarks of the church? Which of the five is most prominent in our churches? Which is least prominent?

(2) Do you agree that, like the ancient people of Athens, modern Americans are enamored with "the new and improved"? How can we reach people like that with an "old, old story"?

(3) Discuss ways we can take the gospel to the marketplace like Paul did in Athens. Do you agree that much modern Christianity is introverted?

(4) Paul's encounter with the silversmiths in Ephesus raises again the issue of economic justice. Are there modern examples of the gospel being compromised so someone can make a profit?

(5) Paul often got discouraged with his own people, the Jews. Do you ever get discouraged with your own people, the church? Are there facets of modern Christianity that embarrass you and make you want to drop out?

(6) Does the Bible ever make you laugh? Do you agree that sometimes we miss biblical humor because we think Scripture has to be somber and serious?

(7) What is the most relevant aspect of Paul's farewell address in Acts 20? Which part of it is most needed by today's church leaders? What can churches do to encourage ministers to be faithful to their covenant with God?

TAKING A STAND (ACTS 21–28)

Focal Text—Acts 26:4-23

Biblical scholar J. Louis Martyn once compared the role of a Bible student to the role of a modern archaeologist. He imagined a team of archaeologists digging up the dusty remains of an especially well-preserved mummy. These archaeologists would be excited about what they might discover about life in another time and place. One thing they would know for sure, though: that mummy, for all of its intrigue, would be dead. Imagine their surprise if this mummy suddenly rose up from the dust, grabbed the spade from the nearest scientist, and hit him over the head with it! Martyn said that, or something like that, is what can happen to the Bible student.

Martyn's point is that the biblical narrative is a living thing. As we study something like the book of Acts, we find that Luke has grabbed the spade from our hands and whacked us in the head. We might have thought we were dealing with a mummy; instead, we tapped into something alive and brimming with energy.

As we have dug around in Acts, we have discovered a group of ordinary people who gathered a most remarkable community. And we have been forced to look at our own communities of faith and wonder if we love each other as much as they did.

We have also uncovered a community that went about the business of breaking down walls. As we read about them embracing the poor and women and Gentiles, we had to ask ourselves if our churches are breaking down any walls.

When we followed Paul on his missionary journeys, spreading the word of Jesus everywhere he went, our own passion was called into question. Are we as bold as Paul? Does the gospel excite us as much as it did him? What can we do to spread the word in our day?

In this final section of our study of Acts, we follow Paul into prison and watch him take a stand for Jesus on a number of occasions. We also go with him to the island of Malta and, finally, to Rome itself. Once again, the mummy will rise up, grab the spade, and whack us in the head. How would we react before these powerful people? Would we take a stand for Jesus under that kind of pressure?

By the time we get to the end of our excavation of Acts, we will know for certain that the mummy is alive. We will be forced to look long and hard at our own church and our own commitment to Jesus Christ. Luke will have given us stories, images, and flesh-and-blood examples that will linger in our memories for a long time.

PAUL RETURNS TO JERUSALEM WHERE HE IS BEATEN AND IMPRISONED (21:1-40)

In the previous session, we left Paul weeping with the Ephesians and heading toward a ship bound for Jerusalem. Paul eventually made it to Jerusalem, but Luke describes a few stops along the way. Paul went to Cos, Rhodes, Patara, and then Tyre, where he stayed a week and had fellowship with the Christians there. The Christians in Tyre warned Paul against going to Jerusalem, but their warning fell on deaf ears. When Paul left Tyre, the scene was similar to the one with the Ephesians. The Tyre Christians—men, women, and children—walked with Paul outside the city, prayed with him, and said farewell. Then Paul boarded another ship and sailed to Ptolemais, where he spent a day with other believers, and then went on to Caesarea.

At Caesarea, he stayed in the home of Philip, one of the original

> **Sea Travel**
>
> Most ships on the Mediterranean were military or cargo vessels. Persons needing to travel by sea would generally hitch a ride on a cargo vessel that was going their direction. Since proceeds from travelers were a secondary source of revenue for the ship owners, travel was relatively inexpensive (about two days' wage for a family). The fare did not include food and there were no cabins for passengers. If the ship hugged the coastline (as was typical) and went into port at night, passengers could disembark and find lodging in local inns, which offered their own dangers, or they could sleep on deck under the stars (see [Inns]). There was always the danger of storms, shipwreck (cf. Acts 27; 2 Cor 11:25), and pirates, though Roman power had dealt rather effectively with the last of these threats.
>
> Everett Ferguson, *Backgrounds of Early Christianity*, 3rd ed. (Grand Rapids MI: Eerdmans, 2003), 86–87.

seven deacons. About twenty years have now passed in Luke's story since Philip had his encounter with the Ethiopian eunuch in Acts 8. Philip had four unmarried daughters who, Luke says, had the gift of prophecy. Here, as he does throughout Acts, Luke offers a subtle reminder that the Way of Jesus is for women, as well as men. Those who argue for the validity of women in ministry find a great ally in Luke and a great resource in the book of Acts.

Paul not only visited with Philip and his daughters; he also received a visit from the prophet Agabus. This is the same Agabus who, in chapter 11, predicted a famine would come upon Judea. Here he predicts that Paul will be imprisoned if he goes to Jerusalem. All of those present, including Luke, urged Paul to listen to Agabus and not go to Jerusalem. Paul, however, was adamant: "For I am ready not only to be bound but even to die in Jerusalem for the name of the Lord Jesus" (Acts 21:13).

Scholars have speculated as to exactly why Paul was so determined to go there. Was he determined to deliver the offering he had gathered for the poor of Jerusalem? Did he want to vindicate his name and ministry? Was he homesick for the "mother church"? Were there specific friends in Jerusalem he wanted, and needed, to see? No one knows for sure. What we do know is that Paul set his face toward Jerusalem, and no prophet or cadre of weeping friends could dissuade him.

Once he got to Jerusalem, things went from bad to worse for Paul. The leaders of the church informed him that many Jewish Christians believed he was too "liberal" in his teachings, that he taught people to forsake Moses, shun circumcision, and ignore Jewish custom. To rectify the situation, they suggested that Paul do something tangible to show his respect for Jewish tradition. Four young men were in the midst of the Nazirite vow, a vow taken in gratitude for some special blessing. This vow involved abstention from meat and wine for thirty days, not cutting one's hair, spending long hours in the temple courts, bringing expensive offerings to the temple, and, finally, shearing one's hair and making an offering of it. Paul was encouraged to join these four in the vow and even to pay for their offerings. That way he would show everyone he really was a practicing Jew, not a liberal heretic.

Paul agreed to do it. E. M. Blaiklock, in his commentary on Acts, thinks the Jerusalem church was wrong to ask Paul to take this vow, and that Paul was wrong to consent to it.[1] Certainly, it must have gone against his instincts. He had moved beyond these kinds of legalistic vows to embrace the radical freedom of Jesus, but, rightly or wrongly, he did agree to try to prove his "Jewishness" to his critics.

Proving his Jewishness did not, however, end his problems. As Paul was completing his Nazirite vow, a group of angry Jews showed up and accused him of heresy. They accused Paul of trampling on their Jewish custom by bringing a Gentile into the temple. Gentiles could go into the Court of the Gentiles, but no further. The crowd said that Paul had brought a Gentile named Trophimus into places where he was not allowed (see page 95, **The Jerusalem Temple**).

Once again, the charge against Paul was that he was blatantly violating Jewish law. The irony of the scene is obvious: there stood Paul, head shorn from his recent Nazirite vow in an attempt to prove his respect for Jewish custom, being accused of not caring about Jewish custom. The moral is obvious too: no matter how hard you try to please, you can never do quite enough.

This crowd was so upset, Luke says, that they wanted to kill Paul and would have killed him had not a group of soldiers and centurions come to his rescue. They dragged Paul away from the angry mob while the people screamed, "Away with him!" (Acts 20:36).

In this chaos, the soldiers had no idea who Paul was or what he had done. They just knew that a riot was breaking out, and their job was to prevent riots. The tribune, or commander, thought Paul was a noted Egyptian rabble-rouser who had given them trouble in the past, but Paul assured him he was a Jew from Tarsus in Cilicia. Then, amazingly, Paul

The Egyptian

The Roman tribune suspected that Paul might be "the Egyptian." The narrator uses the tribune's short address to Paul to inform the reader about this revolutionary. After stirring up a revolt he led 4,000 assassins (see [Sicarii]) into the wilderness (21:38).

The Jewish historian Josephus twice speaks of "the Egyptian" in his historical annals (*Ant.* 20.169–72; *J. W.* 2.261–63). The Egyptian claimed to be a prophet who led 30,000 men (Luke's number of 4,000 seems more realistic) from the desert to the Mount of Olives. From there they were to witness the collapse of the walls, whereupon he and his followers would secure the city. Felix, who served as the procurator from AD 52–60, stopped the effort, killing about 400 of the rebels and capturing around 200. The Egyptian got away.

Josephus's account helps modern readers understand the complex intertwining of religion and politics among first-century Jewish revolutionaries. The trek from the wilderness to the outskirts of the city of Jerusalem, which was to result in the collapse of the walls, was clearly a reenactment of ancient Israel's sojourn through the wilderness and its invasion of the promised land, including the collapse of the walls at Jericho. Many Jews were hoping to experience in their own time a demonstration of God's liberating powers similar to what their ancestors had experienced during the birth of Israel as a nation under Moses and Joshua.

Jesus and Paul

The narrator offers a portrayal of Paul that highlights similarities and parallels between the Lord and the disciple. Charles Talbert lays out the parallels most systematically, only a summary of which is presented:

- Both Jesus' and Paul's final and climactic journeys to Jerusalem receive focused attention (Luke 9:51, 53; 13:22, 33; 17:11; 18:31; 19:11; 19:28; Acts 19:21; 20:22; 21:4, 11-12, 13, 15, 17)
- Both are initially well received (Luke 19:37; Acts 21:17-20a)
- Both go to the temple (Luke 19:45-48; Acts 21:26)

- Both discuss the issue of resurrection, dividing Sadducees and scribes or Pharisees (Luke 20:27-39; Acts 23:6-9)
- Each is the victim of mob action (Luke 22:54; Acts 21:30), which cries "Away with this man [or him]" (Luke 23:18; Acts 21:36)
- Each has four trials or hearings
- Jesus: Sanhedrin (Luke 22:26), Pilate (23:1); Herod (23:8); Pilate (23:13)
- Paul: Sanhedrin (Acts 23); Felix (Acts 24); Festus (Acts 25); Agrippa [a Herodian] (Acts 26)
- Each is declared innocent by government officials (Luke 23:4, 14, 22; Acts 23:9; 25:25; 26:31)

Charles H. Talbert, *Literary Patterns, Theological Themes and the Genre of Luke–Acts* (SBLMS 20; Missoula MT: Scholars Press, 1974), 17–18.

asked for permission to speak to the angry crowd. There is nothing more unreasonable and unkind than a screaming, out-of-control crowd. But Paul insisted he wanted to say a word to this crowd, and the tribune granted him permission. When chapter 21 ends, a hush falls over the crowd as Paul prepares to speak.

Before we hear Paul's address to that angry mob, let's pause and reflect upon chapter 21. Three things stand out as we think about Paul's experiences in this chapter.

First, we notice Paul's determination. Like Jesus, he had set his face toward Jerusalem and was determined to go there, even if it cost him his life. All along the way, people tried to talk him out of going, but, at least in his mind, he was a man on a mission from God.

Second, we notice that everywhere Paul went a band of believers met him and offered him encouragement. In Tyre, Ptolemais, and Caesarea, Christians greeted him, prayed with him, and wept when he departed. It was true then, and it is true now: church, when it is truly the church, is where you go to find love. In an angry, troubled world, Paul had pockets of Christians who embraced him and gave him hope.

Third, we notice again the suffering that Paul had to experience. Perhaps Luke mentions Paul's suffering so often because he wants to correct some misconceptions about discipleship. Willimon writes, "The age of the Spirit has begun at

Pentecost in the resurrection and ascension of Jesus. Yet this does not end sickness, suffering, evil, injustice, ignorance, and rejection . . . . To be empowered by the Spirit cannot mean to be shielded from all heartache and pain. The notion that only good things happen to faithful people was put to rest on a Friday afternoon at Calvary."[2] If that notion didn't vanish when we learned about the cross, it certainly should vanish when we read about Paul's experience in Acts.

PAUL GIVES HIS TESTIMONY TO THE PEOPLE OF JERUSALEM (22:1-30)

Before that silent, seething, crowd Paul gave his testimony of faith. We can pinpoint four basic units of thought in his testimony:

(1) *A description of Paul's training as a zealous Jew* (22:3-5). He was born in Tarsus, studied at the feet of Gamaliel, and was educated in strict Jewish law. To prove his devotion to Jewish law, he persecuted people of the Way and carried them to prison.

(2) *Paul's encounter with Jesus* (22:6-11). While on a journey to Damascus, he had a miraculous encounter with Jesus that transformed his life. But after that encounter on the Damascus Road, Paul was left blind and bewildered by what had happened to him.

(3) *Ananias and his help* (22:12-16). A devout Jew named Ananias came to him in Damascus, restored his sight, and challenged him to tell the world what he had experienced.

(4) *Paul's vision in the temple* (22:17-21). After his return to Jerusalem, he had a vision in the temple telling him to get out of Jerusalem because the people there would not accept his testimony. In the vision, Jesus spoke to him and told him to take the message "far away to the Gentiles" (Acts 22:21).

As soon as Paul said the word "Gentiles," the crowd erupted in anger. What kind of madman was this anyway? Preaching to the Gentiles? God declaring love to Gentiles? Luke says the people were so agitated they shouted, threw off their cloaks, and tossed dust in the air.

Once again the tribune, or commander, came to Paul's rescue and ordered Paul back to the barracks away from the mayhem. But he also ordered Paul to

Paul and Gamaliel

Paul claims in Acts 22:3 to have studied with Gamaliel I. The Paul of the Epistles makes no such claim, implicitly or explicitly. As with so many of the historical and biographical claims of Acts that cannot be confirmed from other sources, scholars are divided as to the veracity of this claim of the Book of Acts.

Lüdemann thinks it "may be . . . historical" that Paul was educated in Jerusalem, but renders no judgment on his having studied with Gamaliel (Lüdemann, 240). Haenchen, following Rudolf Bultmann, argues that the claim is "scarcely correct" since Gal 1:22 implies that Paul was not well known among Judean Christians; therefore, he could not have spent much time in Jerusalem as either a student of Judaism or persecutor of Christians (Haenchen, 625).

N. T. Wright argues that Paul's great zeal, which manifested itself in the violent persecution of Christian Jews whom he perceived to be living in violation of the law, would be consistent with a Pharisee of the more stringent school of Shammai. Gamaliel was of the school of Hillel (in fact, Hillel was his grandfather) and "the Hillelites, broadly speaking, pursued a policy of 'live and let live.' . . . The Shammaites believed that . . . Torah itself . . . demanded that Israel be free from the Gentile yoke, free to serve God in peace, calling no-one master except YHWH, the one true God, himself" (Wright, 27). If Wright's conclusion is correct, one would at least have to deduce that if Paul did once study under Gamaliel, he chose not to follow his "way" of being Jewish. In which case Paul's claim to have studied under the great rabbi, thereby attempting to ride Gamaliel's coattails into the hearts of his audience, is accurate but not wholly truthful.

Gerd Lüdemann, *Early Christianity according to the Traditions in Acts: A Commentary* (Minneapolis: Fortress, 1989); Ernst Haenchen, *The Acts of the Apostles: A Commentary* (Philadelphia: Westminster, 1971); N. T. Wright, *What St. Paul Really Said: Was Paul of Tarsus the Real Founder of Christianity?* (Grand Rapids MI: Eerdmans, 1997).

be whipped, so they could find out why the crowd was so enraged. If they roughed Paul up a bit, perhaps he would confess to his crime.

Paul asked a centurion standing nearby if it was legal to flog a Roman citizen who had been convicted of nothing. That remark set in motion a panic that kept Paul from being punished. The soldiers drew back from him, Luke says, and even the tribune was afraid that he might have done something illegal in arresting Paul. Once they realized Paul was a Roman citizen, everything changed.

What do you do when you don't know what to do? You pass the buck to someone else! The tribune called a meeting of the Jewish Sanhedrin to let those religious leaders decide what to do with Paul, and the next day Paul stood before that august body of the high priest and his cohorts. When chapter 21 ended, Paul was getting ready to speak to the angry crowd in Jerusalem. When chapter 22 ends, Paul stands before the Sanhedrin to take, once again, a stand for Jesus.

The irony in this chapter, and throughout this section of Acts, is that Paul's enemies turn out to be his own people—religious Jews—and his protectors turn out to be calloused Romans simply doing their duty. Religious people persecute him and want his scalp; pagans protect him and enable him to do his evangelistic work. Luke would remind us that life is strange, and God works in mysterious ways.

PAUL SPEAKS TO THE SANHEDRIN AND IS SENT TO CAESAREA TO MEET WITH FELIX, THE GOVERNOR (23:1-34)

Paul obviously wasn't intimidated by the high priest and his cohorts on the Sanhedrin. He began his address by calling them "brothers," which put him on their level and instantly offended them. Ananias, the high priest, struck Paul on the mouth for being so bold, and Paul, still unfazed, lashed back by calling Ananias "a whitewashed wall." So much for good beginnings!

Once Paul began his address to the Sanhedrin, he adopted a wily, diversionary tactic that divided the group on theological issues. The Sanhedrin was made up of both Pharisees and Sadducees, and those groups had a lot of differences. The Pharisees believed in the minutiae of the oral law; the Sadducees believed only in the written law. The Pharisees believed in predestination; the

---

Resurrection of the Dead

Little is said in the Old Testament of this belief. Some statements are actually metaphorical expressions relating to the restoration of the nation of Israel (cf. Isa 26:19; Ezek 37:13-14; Hos 6:1-2). Dan 12:2 (mid-2d century BC) offers the first clear expression of the hope. As evidenced in the conflict of the Sanhedrin in Acts 23:8, there was no uniform belief among Jews regarding afterlife or resurrection. Views seemed to exist within a wide range:

- Sheol was the place of death where one was cut off from God (Sir 17:27–28). There is, effectively, no afterlife in any meaningful sense.
- Belief in immortality of the soul, though such immortality is not understood as an intrinsic property of the soul, but a gift of God, preserved for the righteous (Wis 1–6).
- A resurrection of the righteous, understood quite literally (2 Macc 7): it is implied that mutilated bodies would be restored (2 Macc 14:46). *1 Enoch* seems to envision a resurrection of the righteous, with the evil people being destroyed (*1 En.* 91:10-11).
- A resurrection of both the just and unjust to receive their due rewards (*2 Bar* 50-51; 2 Esd 7:32-44).

George W. E. Nickelsburg, "Resurrection: Early Judaism and Christianity," *ABD* 5.684–91; David Rolph Seely, "Resurrection," *EDB* 1120–22.

Josephus on the Sadducees

"The Sadducees . . . do away with Fate. . . . They maintain that man has the free choice of good or evil. . . . As for the persistence of the soul after death, penalties in the underworld, and rewards, they will have none of them." (*J. W.* 2.164–65)

Sadducees believed in free will. The Pharisees believed in angels and demons; the Sadducees did not. But, most importantly, the Pharisees believed in the resurrection of the dead; the Sadducees did not.

Paul declared himself to be a Pharisee and proceeded to raise the issue of resurrection. The mere mention of the word launched a discussion that quickly degenerated into a catfight. When the Sanhedrin's theological discussion became heated, the ever-present, ever-necessary tribune stepped in to rescue Paul again and get him back to the barracks. (Wouldn't it be wonderful to have our very own tribune to step in and rescue us whenever things get heated in the church?)

The next vignette in Acts 23 shows us two things: the intense anger Paul had aroused in the hearts of his enemies and the impartial justice that lived in the hearts of his protectors. Luke tells us that more than forty Jewish men made a pact to kill Paul. They vowed not to eat again until Paul was dead. It was at this point in the story that Paul's nephew intervened to tell his uncle about this dastardly plot. Paul told the young man to go tell the tribune what he knew, and the tribune, ever faithful to his duty, appointed a squadron of 200 soldiers, 70 horsemen, and 200 spearmen to get Paul out of Jerusalem and on to Caesarea, some 60 miles away.

The tribune, whose name was Claudius Lysias, also sent a letter to Felix, the Roman governor of Judea, informing him of all that had transpired with Paul and expressing his own opinion that Paul was innocent. When Felix read the letter, he agreed to hear Paul's case once his accusers arrived to bring their charges. The date of Paul's arrival in Caesarea was about AD 58, and he would remain there two years.

PAUL GIVES HIS TESTIMONY TO FELIX (24:1-27)

Though Luke doesn't tell us much about Felix, we know a few things about him from other sources. He was the first slave in history to become a Roman governor. He ruled with an iron fist, first in Samaria and then in Judea (AD 52–59). He was married to three princesses, one after another. He was completely

Location of Paul's Imprisonment at Herod's Palace, Caesarea Maritima

Excavation of Caesarea Harbor and Palace. (Credit: Todd Bolen, "Caesarea harbor aerial from west," [cited 20 September 2007]. Online: http://www.bibleplaces.com.)

unscrupulous and capable of almost anything, even hiring assassins to get rid of his detractors. In short, he was a crooked politician and addicted to power. It was before an unsavory character like this that Paul would have to appear and have his case heard.

Five days after Paul arrived in Caesarea, his accusers showed up to bring their charges against him. His prosecutors included Ananias, the high priest;

Felix

Felix governed from c. AD 52–60. He was a former slave and not an able administrator. Even the Roman historian Tacitus characterized him as "practicing every kind of cruelty and lust; he exercised royal power with the instincts of a slave" (*Histories* 5.9). During his administration he had a number of encounters with Jewish revolutionaries. The Jewish terrorist group known as the Sicarii, which specialized in political assassination, was especially active. While Felix made it a point to rid Judea of these and other brigands (Josephus, *J. W.* 2.252), he was willing to conspire with these enemies of the Roman Empire to assassinate the high priest Jonathan, with whom Felix was having serious political disagreements (Josephus, *Ant.* 20.173–78). It was also during this administration that a major disturbance erupted under the leadership of the Egyptian with whom Paul was confused in Acts 22. According to Josephus, it was Felix's forces that killed so many of his followers (*Ant.* 20.169–72). Further, though Felix was assured by Claudius Lysias that Paul was guilty of no political crimes, one can understand why Felix, so accustomed to having to deal with Jewish agitators, would want to look into this case. Acts 24:26 indicates that Felix was hoping that Paul would offer him a bribe in order to secure his release from prison. This is not out of character for Felix.

Nazarenes

Acts 24:5 is the only place in the New Testament where followers of Jesus are referred to as Nazarenes (Gk. *Nazoreans*). Despite there being only one reference in the New Testament, there is evidence from subsequent testimony that the term was used to denote followers of Jesus. Tertullian (c. AD 200) writes that Jews still referred to Christians as "Nazarenes." About 100 years later the church historian Eusebias states that Christians used to be called Nazarenes. Jewish Christians apparently continued to call themselves "Nazarenes," or some close derivation, according to church fathers (who considered Jewish Christianity to be a heresy). Finally, there is evidence that the synagogue used the term *Nosrim* to denote Christians (or, perhaps only Jewish Christians).

Stephen Goranson, "Nazarenes," *ABD* 4.1049–50.

some elders, or members of the Sanhedrin; and a certain attorney/orator named Tertullus. Tertullus, after flattering Felix for being such a great leader, launched into a three-point attack against Paul: (1) he is a pest and agitator, (2) he is a ringleader of the heretical sect known as the Nazarenes, and (3) he has profaned the temple. Those with him agreed and joined in a chorus condemning Paul.

Paul answered those charges by readily admitting that he was a follower of the Way but that he was worshiping the same God his Jewish ancestors worshiped and that everything he believed was a fulfillment of the Jewish Scriptures. He also said he believed in the resurrection, just as his accusers did, and that he tried to keep his conscience clear before God.

Having spoken to each one of the charges brought against him, Paul then proceeded to describe what had really happened in Jerusalem. He had gone there to deliver an offering to the poor. When confronted in the temple, he had been ceremonially pure, having just completed his Nazirite vow. And none of the Asian Jews actually present on that occasion were now present before Felix to level any charges against him.

Felix, whom Luke says was rather well informed about the Way, adjourned the hearing with no comment and simply said he would consult with the tribune, Claudius Lysias, before rendering a verdict. Then Felix ordered the centurion to keep Paul in custody but to allow him certain freedoms, like letting his friends come to him and meet his needs.

After that, Felix would consult with Paul often and converse with him, hoping to extract a bribe from him. Paul used those occasions to discuss "justice, self-control, and the coming judgment" (Acts 24:25), which, understandably, made Felix nervous. With what he knew of his past, no wonder he was frightened when Paul spoke to him of those things!

Two years passed, and nothing happened. Paul never had a trial. Paul never offered a bribe. Claudius was never consulted. For all practical purposes, Paul got lost in the bureaucratic shuffle of Felix's incompetence. When, after years of such incompetence, the Jews asked the emperor for a new governor, Felix was replaced by Portius Festus.

It was the custom to release unconvicted prisoners when there was a change of governors, but, in one final act of bumbling, Felix, in a desperate attempt to please the Jews, left Paul in prison. So, with this episode, Felix passes from the pages of the Bible and the annals of history as a figure of shame.

PAUL MEETS WITH FESTUS, THE NEW GOVERNOR (25:1-27)

You might think that after two years, the Jews in Jerusalem would have forgotten all about Paul and moved on to other things. But that was not the case. Just three days into his regime as governor of Judea, Festus took a trip from Caesarea to Jerusalem and got an earful from Paul's enemies there. The Jews in Jerusalem were still agitated, still on the warpath. They requested that Paul be transferred back to Jerusalem to stand trial there.

But Festus was a Roman, with a Roman's sense of justice. He was cut out of a different bolt of cloth than Felix and wouldn't bow to Paul's detractors. He said Paul would stay in Caesarea and, if they wanted to pursue the case against him, they would have to go there. Festus would die after two brief years as governor and his impact on history would be small, but he comes across in Acts as a just, upright leader.

After a brief stay in Jerusalem, Festus returned to Caesarea. Paul's accusers were close on his heels. The day after Festus returned, he took his seat on the tribunal and had Paul brought before him. The Jews from Jerusalem brought "many serious charges against him" (Acts 25:7), which, Luke adds, they could

---

Festus

Porcius Festus assumed the office of governor (or procurator) c. AD 60 and ruled until c. AD 62. According to Josephus, he made conscientious attempts to deal with anti-Roman insurgents, particularly the assassination squads, known as the *sicarii*. "Now it was that Festus succeeded Felix as procurator, and made it his business to correct those that made disturbances in the country. So he caught the greatest part of the robbers, and destroyed a great many of them" (Josephus, *J. W.* 2.271; cf. *Ant.* 20.188).

Appealing to Caesar

Historically, evidence indicates that the right of Roman citizens to appeal to the Emperor was absolute. Witherington's quotation of Paulus, *Sent.* 5.26.1, is self-explanatory:

> Anyone invested with authority who puts to death or orders to be put to death, tortures, scourges, condemns, or directs a Roman citizen who first appealed to the people, and now has appealed to the Emperor, to be placed in chains, shall be condemned under the Lex Julia relating to public violence. The punishment of his crime is death, where the parties are of inferior station; deportation to an island where they are of superior station.

Given this, it would seem that, historically, Festus had no option but to grant Paul's appeal. Readers should assume that a Roman-appointed procurator would have known this, leaving Festus's consultation with his council (25:12)

something of a mystery. Of course, one could argue that Festus was not really sure what the legal ramifications were, explaining why he sought counsel.

Modern readers should not anachronistically assume the contemporary situation of American jurisprudence, where the often-exorbitant costs of appeals are regularly assumed by the state, particularly for defendants who "cannot afford an attorney." In Roman jurisprudence, the defendant had to assume all costs of the appeal, including her or his own transportation to Rome. Talbert notes, "The appellant would personally have to undertake the costs of travel to Rome, the living expenses while there, and perhaps the costs of actually litigating the case, including securing witnesses" (210).

Ben Witherington III, *The Acts of the Apostles: A Socio-Rhetorical Commentary* (Grand Rapids MI: Eerdmans, 1998), 725; Charles H. Talbert, *Reading Acts: A Literary and Theological Commentary of the Acts of the Apostles* (New York: Crossroad, 1997).

---

not prove. Paul, in his defense, maintained that he had committed no crime against Jewish law, the temple, or Caesar.

Festus asked if Paul would be willing to go to Jerusalem to be tried there if he, Festus, served as judge. But Paul had had all of the bureaucratic red tape he could stand. After all, he had been in prison in Caesarea for two years already, and nothing had been done. So Paul turned down Festus's plan for a Jerusalem trial and appealed his case to the emperor.

Every Roman citizen had that right. If a person felt justice was not being served in a local province, that person could appeal to the emperor in Rome. Only murderers, pirates, and bandits caught in the act were denied the appeal. So Paul, as a Roman citizen, had a valid appeal, and Festus, under Roman law, had no choice: "You have appealed to the emperor; to the emperor you will go" (Acts 25:12).

There was only one hitch. When a local leader sent a person to the emperor, that leader also had to send along the charges against that person. Festus's problem was simple: he couldn't think of any crime Paul had committed. How could he send Paul to Caesar if there were no charges against him?

Fortunately for Festus, King Agrippa and his sister, Bernice, came to Caesarea to welcome him as the new governor, and Festus asked Agrippa to help him draft a set of charges to send to Rome. Luke sets up a dramatic scene where the leaders of Caesarea are present in a large room, and the king and his sister enter to much pomp and fanfare. Then Paul is brought in, bound in his chains, as a lowly prisoner.

Agrippa

Marcus Julius Agrippa was born in AD 27 or 28, the son of Agrippa I (referred to as King Herod in Acts 12). Upon the death of his father in AD 44, Rome thought it best, owing to Agrippa's adolescence, not to allow him to succeed his father, whose kingdom had expanded to the approximate size of that of Herod I (Herod the Great). At the age of 22 (c. AD 50), he was given the kingdom of Chalcis. Around the year 53, however, this was exchanged for the former territory of his great uncle Philip, the son of Herod (the territory to the northeast of Galilee). Later, perhaps around the mid-50s, he was given rule over limited areas of Galilee and Peraea. Agrippa also had appointive powers for the office of high priest. Though, as a Jew, Agrippa was sensitive to Jewish concerns, he was unswervingly loyal to Rome and attempted to intervene to stop the revolt against Rome that would erupt by the end of decade of the 60s, several years after the encounter with Paul about which Acts 25–26 speaks.

David C. Braund, "Agrippa," *ABD* 1.98–100.

As the chapter closes, Paul once again is taking a stand for Christ, this time before Festus and Agrippa.

PAUL GIVES HIS TESTIMONY TO FESTUS AND KING AGRIPPA (26:1-32)

Think for a moment about the scenes Luke has shown us in this last section of Acts. At the end of chapter 21, Paul faced that angry crowd in Jerusalem, ready to defend himself and his faith in Jesus. At the end of chapter 22, Paul appeared before the Sanhedrin, ready to take a stand before those religious leaders. At the end of chapter 23, Paul was getting ready to defend himself and his faith before Felix, the governor. At the end of chapter 24, Paul was getting ready to speak to Festus, the new governor of Judea. And at the end of chapter 25, Paul was getting ready to speak a word of defense to both Festus and Agrippa in the regal setting of that room in Caesarea. Time after time, Luke has shown Paul taking a stand, defending both himself and his Lord.

As chapter 26 opens, Paul speaks to Festus and Agrippa and, once again, tells his story. One thing we know for certain: Luke wants us to know the story of Paul's conversion. This is the third time in Acts we have heard the details of his testimony. In chapter 9, Luke gave us his version of the story. In chapter 22, Paul repeated the story to the angry crowd in Jerusalem. And now in chapter 26, he tells it again to Festus and Agrippa.

Paul tells about his previous life as a Pharisee and persecutor of Christians. He describes his miraculous encounter with Jesus on the Damascus Road. And he reiterates his determination to be true to God's call and share the good news of Jesus with the world.

When Paul finishes his testimony in Acts 26, Festus exclaims that Paul must be out of his mind. Too much learning has pushed him over the edge, he says. Agrippa, for his part, is amazed that Paul would try to make a Christian out of someone like him. But though Festus and Agrippa both seem to sneer at Paul's story, they also agree that Paul has done nothing to deserve death or imprisonment. Agrippa even adds the final irony to the scene: if Paul hadn't appealed his case to the emperor, they would have set him free.

What is noteworthy about this passage is *how* Paul told his story to those government leaders. Since this is the third time we've heard the story, and since it is obvious that Luke makes Paul's conversion a recurring theme in Acts, we might pause a moment and consider Acts 26:4-23 as our focal text for this last section of Acts. Perhaps in noticing how Paul told his story, we can learn a few things about how to tell ours.

Let's begin with an honest, but painful, admission: Christian testimonies are usually "canned" and unappealing. When some smiling soul on "Christian television" launches into a syrupy testimony about how Jesus has changed his life, we usually reach for the remote and try to find a ball game. Christian testimonies typically sound about as authentic as sales pitches for oceanfront property in Arizona.

The typical testimony has a pattern to it:

• I was miserable and having all kinds of problems.
• Then I found Jesus, and he saved me.
• Now I'm happy, and my problems have disappeared.

While that might sound inviting to anyone who is miserable and having all kinds of problems, it doesn't exactly square with the testimony of Paul.

First, notice that Paul never used his own happiness as a component in his conversion story. He gave no indication that he was miserable before his Damascus

Road experience and no indication that he suddenly found happiness after his Damascus Road experience. Unlike modern people, Paul did not see his relationship with Jesus in terms of self-fulfillment.

To Paul, the idea that a relationship with Jesus eliminates problems and produces bliss would have seemed absurd. After all, he gave his testimony to Festus and Agrippa in chains. He had been ridiculed, beaten, stoned, imprisoned, and nearly assassinated. I think it is fair to say that he didn't really know what problems were until he met Jesus!

Willimon imagines what would happen if Paul appeared on a modern-day Christian talk show:

> The "Christian Talk Show" host smiled and said, "We are so thrilled to have a famous Christian with us today to share his testimony with us—Saint Paul!" (*Enthusiastic applause.*)
>
> "Tell us, Paul—or should I call you 'Saint,' which do you prefer?"
>
> "Paul, just Paul the Pharisee would be fine, Jim."
>
> "Great! Paul, tell us about all the wonderful things that happened to you when the Lord Jesus came into your life."
>
> "Well, let's see. First I was struck blind. I got over that but then somebody tried to kill me and I had to escape in a basket. Then they stoned me and . . . ."[3]

I'm not sure Paul would be a hit on most Christian talk shows. Suffering simply doesn't "sell."

It is almost impossible to read this last section of Acts without thinking of Jesus' suffering. As Paul appears before the government authorities, echoes of Jesus' passion and death are everywhere. Both Paul and Jesus go to Jerusalem ready to suffer and die to do the will of God. Both appear before the Sanhedrin, a Roman procurator, and a governor. Both hear the crowd cry, "Away with him!" Both are declared several times to be innocent. Both are beaten. And both experience horrible injustice. Paul truly "suffered for the name," and his journey with Jesus makes most modern testimonies sound like pious fluff.

Second, notice that nowhere in his story does Paul claim to have "found Jesus." Evidently, he had no desire to find Jesus at all. He was merrily going along, being a serious Pharisee and persecutor of heretics when *Jesus found him.* As Willimon writes, "The initiative in all these stories of change and turning around is God's. Luke would know nothing of our smug declarations of spiritual expertise which believes that I found Jesus, I took Jesus into my life, or I gave my life to Christ. For Luke, most of the traffic on the bridge between us and God is coming toward us."[4]

Third, notice that Paul's story was validated by a life of sacrifice. He didn't start a ministry that made him wealthy. He didn't travel in luxury on other people's money. He didn't adopt a philosophy of entitlement that made him snobbish. Paul just went to work. He established churches. He took offerings for the poor. He taught in houses. He stayed with friends. He traveled tirelessly telling the good news. And, as we have seen over and over, he suffered for the name.

When we put Paul's testimony alongside those we hear on Christian television, the differences are dramatic. The three qualities of Paul's testimony stand in stark contrast to modern testimonies.

Modern testimonies tend to be about *my* happiness, *my* fulfillment, and victory over *my* problems. Paul had none of that in his testimony. His story began with miracle and ended with suffering. No respectable advertising executive would have used Paul to sell Christianity. His story wasn't "positive" enough.

Modern testimonies tend to be haughty and egotistical. *I* found Jesus. *I* discovered the truth. *I* experienced joy. Paul said he was simply bowled over on the road to Damascus. It was all of God.

Modern testimonies often are followed by shallow lives of luxury and self-indulgence. Paul not only "talked the talk." He "walked the walk." The sermons he preached in Acts were good. The sermons he *lived* in Acts were even better.

All of this is to remind us that on those rare occasions when we tell our story, and on those frequent occasions when we live our story, we need to learn from Paul.

It's not about how we became successful. It's about being faithful to God through all the ups and downs of life.

It's not about how we found God. It's about how God found us and how amazed we are by God's grace.

It's not about settling into a God-blessed life of ease and luxury. It's about doing tangible deeds of sacrificial love for Jesus' sake.

PAUL IS SENT TO ROME BUT SUFFERS STORM AND SHIPWRECK (27:1-44)

Because Paul had appealed his case to the emperor, arrangements were made for him and some other prisoners to be transported to Rome (see page 96, **Paul's Voyage to Rome**). Acts 27 describes that journey, and what a journey it was!

Acts 27:9 sets an ominous tone for the journey: "Since much time had been lost and sailing was now dangerous, because even the Fast had already gone by, Paul advised them, 'Sirs, I can see that the voyage will be with danger and much heavy loss, not only of the cargo and the ship, but also of our lives.'" The Fast is a reference to the Jewish Day of Atonement in September-October, so we know that this was in the fall of the year (probably AD 60). According to the navigational practice of the time, sailing was deemed dangerous by September and suicidal by November. Paul knew it was not wise to set sail on the Mediterranean Sea at that time of year, but his advice was ignored.

The way Luke describes the voyage, it had four distinct stages—(1) Caesarea to Myra (Acts 27:2-5), (2) Myra to Fair Havens (Acts 27:6-8), (3) Fair

---

History and Paul's Voyage

Unless one assumes either that Paul never actually went to Rome or, if he did, he went by land, then even the greatest skeptic must conclude that, at its core, the story of the sea voyage is historical. That is, Paul sailed to Rome.

As is regularly the case in the critical reading of Acts, views regarding the historicity of the narrative of Acts 27 vary almost as widely as the Mediterranean Sea itself. Lüdemann argues that the narrative "is a literary entity, the result of his reading to which Luke has added the person of Paul" (259). Verses 6-44 "probably have no point of reference in history. . . . In all probability Paul did not suffer any shipwreck before Malta on his last journey to Rome . . ." (260). Similar to the position of Lüdemann, at least with regard to historicity, is that of Dibelius, who argues that Luke took over a separate account of a sea voyage and ship-wreck and inserted Paul in various places (107).

Other interpreters argue that the account is essentially historical, rooted in the report and memory of an eyewitness (Luke), though one may adopt this position and still concede that Luke employed stylized and popular literary devices to make the story as vivid as possible (Witherington, 755–56). Luke Johnson, in some measure, straddles the sea of opinion, granting Luke a very free and creative hand, while reminding readers that the employment of "fictional" literary techniques does not mean "that the events were created entirely out of the author's imagination" (457). Apparently, Johnson is affirming a voyage, a storm, and a shipwreck—a historical event that Luke narrates with considerable literary artistry and freedom.

Gerd Lüdemann, *Early Christianity according to the Traditions in Acts: A Commentary* (Minneapolis: Fortress, 1989); Martin Dibelius, *Studies in the Acts of the Apostles* (Mifflintown PA: Sigler Press, 1999); Ben Witherington III, *The Acts of the Apostles: A Socio-Rhetorical Commentary* (Grand Rapids MI: Eerdmans, 1998); Luke Timothy Johnson, *The Acts of the Apostles* (SacPag 5; Collegeville MN: Liturgical Press, 1992).

Breaking Bread in Acts 27

The following table demonstrates the presence of language in Acts 27:35 and the meals in the Gospel of Luke where Jesus was present.

Acts 27:35	Luke 9:16	Luke 22:19	Luke 24:30
After he had said this, he took bread; and giving thanks to God in the presence of all, he broke it and began to eat.	And taking the five loaves and the two fish, he looked up to heaven, and blessed and broke them, and gave them to the disciples to set before the crowd.	Then he took a loaf of bread, and when he had given thanks, he broke it and gave it to them, saying, "This is my body, which is given for you. Do this in remembrance of me."	When he was at the table with them, he took bread, blessed and broke it, and gave it to them.

Building on the language of the gospel narrative, the "breaking of bread" serves in Acts as a shorthand way of referring to fellowship, implicitly at least, in the presence of Jesus (Acts 2:42, 46; 20:7, 11). In this final reference to the breaking of bread, perhaps significantly, the fellowship that is shared is not exclusive to Christians, but is inclusive of all.

Havens to Malta (Acts 27:9–28:10), and (4) Malta to Rome (Acts 28:11-16). On the third leg of that trip, a violent storm hit the Mediterranean and wreaked havoc on Paul and his fellow voyagers. The storm raged for two solid weeks, leaving everyone fearful and desperate. In fact, Luke reports, "When neither sun nor stars appeared for many days, and no small tempest raged, all hope of our being saved was at last abandoned" (Acts 27:20).

In this whole chaotic storm scene, Luke's eye is riveted on Paul. Paul is the center of the story, in effect the captain of the ship. He is the one encouraging the downcast sailors to take heart. He is the one predicting no lives will be lost. He is the one inviting everyone on board to eat something. (The way Luke relates the story, it sounds like a nautical Lord's Supper. Paul takes bread, blesses it, breaks it, and begins to eat. Somewhere in this text there is a Lord's Supper sermon waiting to happen: taking the supper in the midst of a storm.) There were 276 men on board that ship, but, for Luke's purposes, we only need to look at one of them.

By the end of chapter 27, the ship has struck a reef, the force of the waves has broken the stern, and everyone on board has been forced to swim to shore, or float to shore on planks or other pieces of the ship. Amazingly, all 276 make it safely to land.

New Testament scholar F. F. Bruce calls Luke's account of this voyage "a small classic in its own right."[5]

St. Paul's Bay
This bay is traditionally the site of the shipwreck that left Paul and 275 other persons stranded on Malta. Today it is a bustling resort, offering accommodations that Paul and his ship-wrecked companions could not even have imagined.

View over St. Paul's Bay in Lindos (Island of Rhodos), Greece (Credit: Angelika Stern, istockphoto.com)

PAUL LANDS ON THE ISLAND OF MALTA BUT EVENTUALLY MAKES IT TO ROME (28:1-31)

"After we had reached safety, we then learned that the island was called Malta" (Acts 28:1). For three months, Paul and his 275 shipmates would stay on the island of Malta and receive unusual kindness by the people there. From that three-month stay, Luke chooses to report only two incidents: (1) Paul getting bitten by a snake but having no ill effect (Acts 28:2-6), and (2) Paul healing Publius, the leader of the island, and many others (Acts 28:7-10).

After three months, the shipwrecked voyagers, loaded with farewell gifts from the islanders, boarded a ship that had wintered at Malta and set sail for Rome. Luke gives us the precise stops along the way—Syracuse, Rhegium, Puteoli, and, finally, Rome. Between Puteoli and Rome, Luke writes, some Christians from Rome came to welcome Paul (and probably to escort him into the city). They traveled a distance of about forty miles to greet him and showed, once again, that though Paul had bitter enemies, he also had loyal friends.

"When he came to Rome, Paul was allowed to live by himself, with the soldier who was guarding him" (Acts 28:16). What happens next is both

Malta

The large island is located sixty miles south of Sicily. The name *Malta* is from the Semitic word melit, which means refuge. It provided "safe harbor" for more than Paul and his fellow travelers down through history. Before coming under Roman rule in 218 BC, Malta had been a Phoenician trading colony for centuries. Punic/Phoenician language and culture remained deeply embedded on the island, even centuries after coming under Roman rule.

W. Ward Gasque, "Malta," *ABD* 4.489–90.

Via Appia

Also known in translation as the Appian Way, this was the most important road through Italy in the days of the empire. It ran from the "heel" of the boot of Italy, across the peninsula in a northwest direction, turning north toward Rome just north of Puteoli. It was here that Paul would have picked up the road to lead him to the city of Rome. It fell out of use with the fall of the empire. A new road was built in the late eighteenth century that roughly parallels the "old Appian Way" (*Via Appia Antica*). Some sections of the old road are still in use.

Appian Way Mist
(Credit: istockphoto.com)

touching and sad. Paul seeks out local Jews to tell them the good news and to win them to Christ. He has said before that he was fed up with the Jews and would limit his efforts to the Gentiles, but he can't keep from wanting his own people to embrace the story of Jesus. Try as he might, he can't give up on the Jews.

He calls them together and tries to persuade them to believe, but to no avail. A few believe, but many do not, and a dispute breaks out among them.

The City of Rome

This is a view of the city of Rome from the SW. The circular building is the famous Coliseum (the Flavian Amphitheater). The elliptically shaped building is the Circus Maximus, famous for chariot races. Paul would have approached from the south on the Appian Way. On the southern edge of the city, the Appian Way merged with *Via Latina* and became

Model of Ancient Rome. (Credit: Todd Bolen, "Rome Model view north," [cited 20 September 2007]. Online: http://www.bibleplaces.com.)

Via Nova. *Via Nova* headed directly toward Circus Maximus. There is no way to know where in Rome Paul stayed or if he even entered the heart of the city.

Paul, in frustration, quotes Isaiah 6:9-10, a passage about people whose hearts are dull and whose ears are hard of hearing. Once again, he declares that the Gentiles are more willing to hear and embrace the story of Jesus.

Then, suddenly, Luke puts down his pen and ends his story. Just like that, the story is over. The ending seems abrupt and unsatisfying: "He lived there two whole years at his own expense and welcomed all who came to him, proclaiming the kingdom of God and teaching about the Lord Jesus Christ with all boldness and without hindrance" (Acts 28:30-31).

When the Acts story ends, Paul is still being Paul—living at his own expense, welcoming believers and seekers, and proclaiming the kingdom of God and telling about Jesus "with all boldness," as he always had. When the book of Acts ends, Paul, who has spent the last few years of his life taking a stand before angry crowds and Sanhedrins and government officials, is still taking a stand for Jesus.

CONCLUSION

The ending of Acts seems unsatisfying because we yearn to know what happened to Paul. Did he die there in Rome? Or was he eventually set free to travel more and share the gospel? After following Paul as he appeared before Felix, Festus, and Agrippa, shouldn't we get to see him before Caesar? From one perspective, it seems that Luke shortchanged us when he ended his story so abruptly with Paul still in that Roman prison.

But from another perspective, Luke's ending makes perfect sense. After all, it was not his purpose in Acts to give us Paul's biography; it was his purpose to tell the story of the church, how it started with a handful of people and swept the world. Luke wanted to chronicle those thirty years that changed the world.

The other reason the ending makes sense is that it is so open-ended. Luke ends the story as if there is more action to come. Nothing is tied down. Many questions have yet to be answered. The church is still growing and changing. Paul is still declaring the good news. When you finish reading Acts, you get the sense that there is definitely going to be a sequel.

From that perspective, it is a brilliant ending and, perhaps, Luke's intention. What happened during those thirty years that changed the world was amazing, but the story isn't over. The church is alive, growing, and changing. What happens next is yet to be determined.

Will the Spirit come again in miracle and power as in Acts 2? Will God raise up another Paul? Will Christians continue to deal with suffering as courageously as the Acts Christians? What new challenges will arise to test the character and courage of Jesus' followers? Will the church continue to gather a community, break down walls, spread the word, and take a stand like the church in Acts did?

When we finish our study of Acts, there is one thing we *do* know for certain: you and I, and your church and mine, will get to live out the answers to those questions.

NOTES

[1] See E. M. Blaiklock, *Acts: The Birth of the Church* (Old Tappan NJ: Fleming H. Revell Company, 1980), 219–20.

[2] William Willimon, *Acts*, Interpretation Commentary (Atlanta: John Knox Press, 1988), 160–61.

[3] Willimon, *Acts*, 180.

[4] Ibid.

[5] F. F. Bruce, *Commentary on the Book of Acts*, New International Commentary of the New Testament (Grand Rapids MI: William B. Eerdmans, 1959), 498.

QUESTIONS FOR REFLECTION AND DISCUSSION

(1) Why do you think Paul was so determined to go to Jerusalem? Have you ever made a decision regardless of the protests of your friends and family? How did it turn out?

(2) With which part of Paul's testimony do you most identify? Can you think of a modern testimony that has influenced you? Are most modern testimonies canned and unappealing? What makes a testimony powerful?

(3) Do you agree that saints sometimes wound us worse than sinners? How do you account for that fact? Why does God seem to lead Christian people in such different directions?

(4) Does the ending of Acts seem unsatisfactory to you? Why do you think Luke ended the book so abruptly? What do you think eventually happened to Paul?

(5) At what point in our study of Acts did the mummy rise up, grab the spade, and hit you in the head? What one truth in the book spoke most to you or most convicted you? What specific new truth did you learn from the study?

APPENDIX:
MAPS & DIAGRAMS

Jerusalem in the First Century

In this detailed model of ancient Jerusalem one can see in the far upper right-hand corner the temple area where Acts says early Christians gathered daily (2:46). The tall building in the upper center with pyramid-apex is the tomb of David to which Peter makes reference (2:29; see **Map of Jerusalem**). To the left of the tomb is the Palace of Caiaphas. Readers might imagine some scenes where priestly authorities question the apostles as taking place here, but one cannot be sure.

(Credit: Jim Pitts)

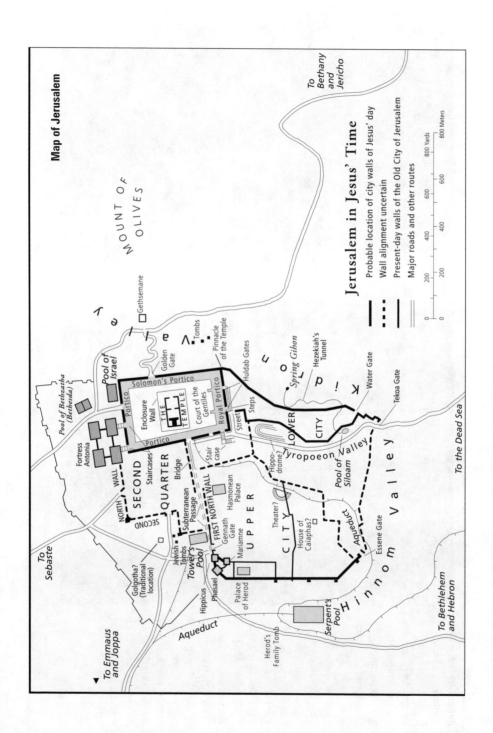

Map of Jerusalem

Map of Palestine in New Testament Times

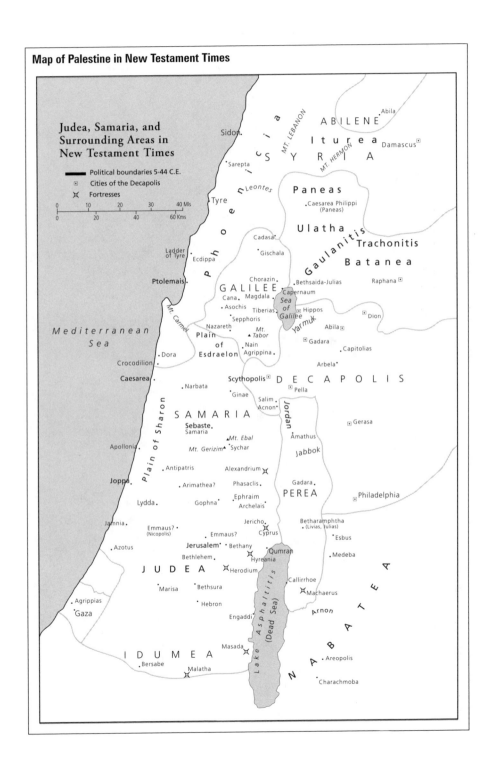

Map of Paul's First Missionary Journey

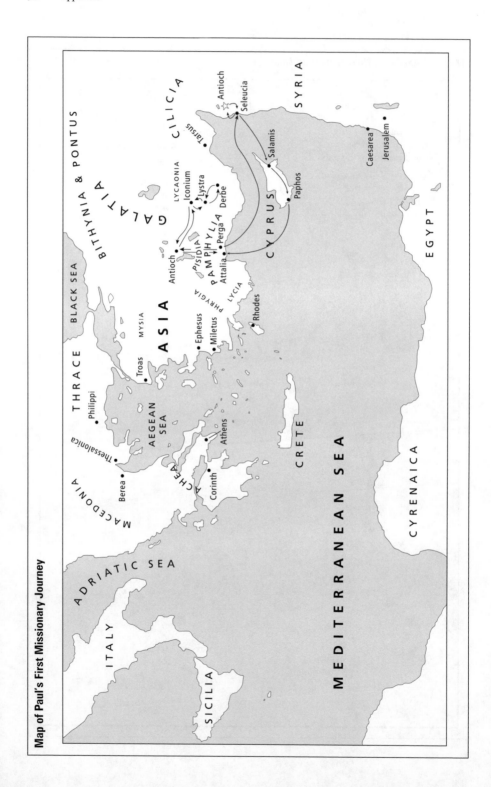

Map of Paul's Second Missionary Journey

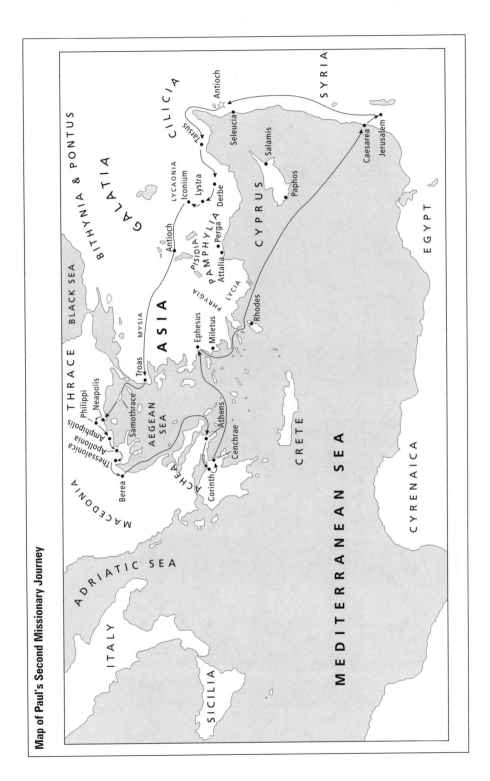

Map of Paul's Third Missionary Journey

Paul's so-called third missionary journey is narrated in Acts 18:23–20:38, beginning from Antioch of Syria. At the conclusion of this "journey" Paul set sail for Jerusalem, arriving there in Acts 21:17.

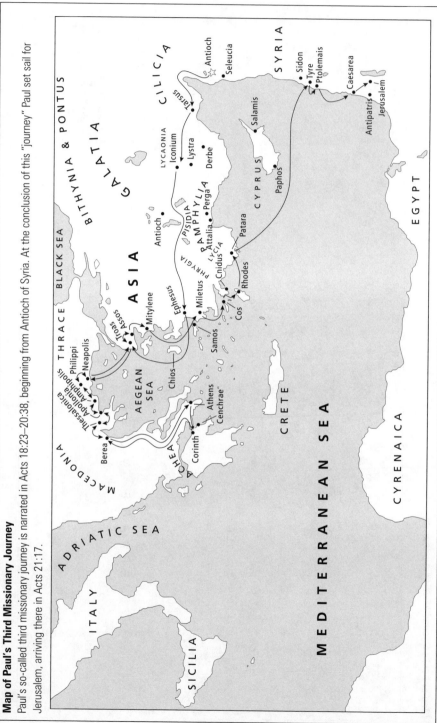

The Jerusalem Temple

The Jerusalem temple increasingly restricted access the closer one came to the holy of holies. Note in the diagram of the temple that the Court of the Gentiles is in the outermost areas, *outside* the inner courts. The first inner court is that of the Court of Women. Looking at the model of the Jerusalem temple (here one is looking at the temple from the East), the Court of Women is the first "inner court," located in the bottom portion of the picture. The gates entering into the Court of Women may be the "doors" or "gates" that "were shut" (21:30). At the end of the Court of Women, one can see steps leading up to a second gate (this is the Nicanor Gate and, possibly, the Beautiful Gate to which Acts 3:2 refers). Beyond this is the Court of Israel, where men were permitted to view the work of priests in the Court of Priests, just outside and in front of the Sanctuary (*naos*) proper. The Sanctuary proper represents even holier space, with access restricted to priests who, by lot, were assigned roles within the Sanctuary (see Luke 1:8-9). Within the Sanctuary was the holy of holies, into which the high priest would enter on the Day of Atonement.

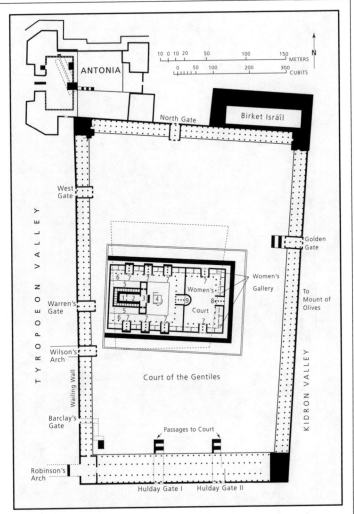

Paul's Voyage to Rome

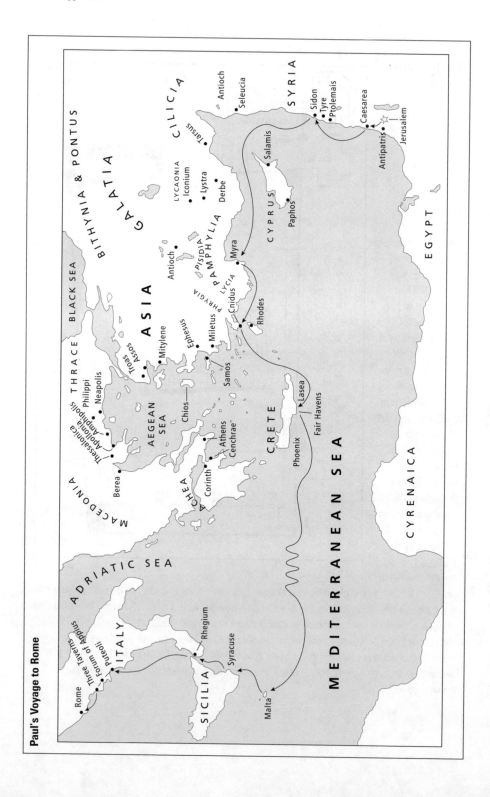